MAITREY

Sisterhood
of the Dove
Clarion Call of Mary Magdalene

Outskirts Press, Inc.
Denver, Colorado

Sisterhood of the Dove
Clarion Call of Mary Magdalene
All Rights Reserved.
Copyright © 2008 Maitreya Zohar
V6.0

Cover Photo: Mount of Olives, Jerusalem, Israel – some believe these olive trees were present in the Garden 2000 years ago.
Artwork: Leila Mary Mitchenall - leilamitchenall@yahoo.co.uk

Outskirts Press, Inc.
http://www.outskirtspress.com

ISBN: 978-1-4327-1402-4

Outskirts Press and the "OP" logo are trademarks belonging to Outskirts Press, Inc.

PRINTED IN THE UNITED STATES OF AMERICA

We share this tale with beloved Mother Earth and
all living things.

GRATITUDE

To the Spirit of Mary Magdalene, or Miriyam, as she is called in Hebrew, and to the soul-group of 44: the words *thank you* do not convey the depth of my gratitude. Thank you from the depths of my soul for tending to this beautiful Garden we call Earth.

To my dearest true friend, Ortalia, this writing would not be if it were not for your commitment, service, and love. You contributed countless hours to this project and your name belongs on the front cover with mine. You are terrific and may all you have offered to the world, and me, come back to you more than 1000-fold.

To ChristiElla, who typed many of the original, handwritten notes, supported with proofreading and sat with me on several occasions going over various aspects of the tale. You aided me with healing sessions and vibrational support. For this I say, "I love you."

To my daughter Michal, who touched up the artwork, gave invaluable support, and believed in me.

To Kathryn, who encouraged me to read this tale aloud to her and in so doing, she added a valuable multidimensional listening and depth.

To my dog, Francis, who on many occasions was willing to wait for her walk and her food, as I was deep within the tale, you are missed. Francis died just before this tale was published.

To Madhavi, Odetta, and Keenya for reading the initial manuscript and presenting me with constructive support.

To Debbie, who edited take two, made suggestions I would never have imagined, and connected me with my first potential publisher.

To Kari, who infused new life into each character as she completed editing Miriyam's journey with me, I am moved, touched, and inspired by your gift.

To Leila, your artwork is deeply appreciated.

To Janet, thanks for interviewing me on your radio show and proofreading this tale.

To Carol, your encouragement of me brings such peace and joy. I love you.

PREFACE

The ways of Oral Teachings are not as common as they once were. Not long ago, Orators, gifted men and women learned in the art of communication, passed teachings from one generation to the next through storytelling. Each story had within it several layers of teachings, allowing groups of all ages to partake. The listeners received the teachings as they were ready to accept them. A gifted Orator communicated a story with 10 different levels of teachings.

There is a power in Oral Traditions and Oral Teachings that the Mystery Schools use and is hidden in our modern society. Oral transmissions-- what some people call *channeling* today--bring Spirit into the material world. This energy of Spirit is referred to by names like *Chi* or *Shakti* in other cultures. In our modern culture, some of this energy of Spirit is missing in the quest for knowledge over wisdom. It is this quest for knowledge that "kicked us out of the Garden," according to Biblical teachings.

Sisterhood of the Dove was written with many layers of text to speak to the reader who is interested in hearing the tale as it might be told to children. It was also written for the reader who is interested in knowledge, and in evolving the soul. The Spirit of the Dove, *Shekenah*--Holy Spirit--lives in this tale. As Miriyam, or Mary Magdalene, evolves in the telling, the reader, too, is offered the opportunity to evolve.

The reader who absorbs its many layers will be transformed by the energy of the Dove.

The healing of fear, jealousy, power, and control is at the core of this tale.

As the author, I recommend you read this tale at least three times and have someone read it to you once. The first time you read the teachings, your mental body will be touched; your mind will be involved, trying to figure out what is being said: Asking questions, criticizing, judging how the teachings were presented, and more.

The second reading will invoke your emotional body. The words seem more familiar. Your mind will have a degree of understanding and your energy will begin to flow toward your heart. You will open to the possibility of feeling your way through the teachings.

During the third reading, deeper understanding will take place within your mind; the space created by the emotional clearing of the second reading will begin to fill with the energy of this transmission: in this tale that is the Dove. This action will bring the teachings into your physical body.

Listening to the teachings will enroll your inner child, your innocent one who is full of trust and faith. With your *little one* enrolled, your paradigm will shift. And when your paradigm shifts, you will naturally find yourself enthusiastically sharing your newly embodied teachings with the world around you.

*   *   *   *   *

On July 22, 2003 the Feast Day of Mary Magdalene, Mary channeled through Shoshana/Ortalia Rogers, giving the inspiration for this tale to a group of about 14 people. Mary allowed each person to ask questions regarding her time on Earth some 2000 years ago.

During the group experience, I heard Mary communicating from within me as well as through Ortalia. This was not unusual for me but I was surprised because at that time I was unaware of my intimate connection with Mary.

Two days passed and the words *Sisterhood of the Dove* entered my mind. "What a great name for a book," I thought.

This, too, was odd because, as a writer of many short stories, I have always received the title of each story upon its completion. This meant that the book had already been written about Mary. It was somewhere in the ethers, and needed to be brought forth.

I went back to Ortalia and told her of the name, *Sisterhood of the Dove.* Ortalia loved the title and in time, with coaxing, she agreed to channel Mary. We audio taped the session. Shortly thereafter, Ortalia agreed to allow Mary to communicate that which she desired to share.

In our first meeting dedicated to writing, I asked Mary, "There are so many books, why another?"

"There are many stories about me out there," she said. "It matters not; this is the one I want you to tell." From there, her dictation began. I asked questions only near the end of each session. I observed Mary's body language; I noticed when she would speak in an unconditionally loving way, almost heavenly, about planet Earth and her changes. She allowed me to look deep into her as she showed me a side of humanity that, at the time, I was afraid to touch. She presented every human emotion to me as she recalled her journey with the ones she had loved and the ones she had hated; the ones who had abused her and the ones who had brought her to complete healing in wholeness.

As I transcribed her words from audiotape to paper and from paper to computer, the Spirit of the Dove flowed through me and it became clear to me that I would write from the perspective of Mary's fourth born child, Rachel.

This tale asks the reader to imagine himself or herself in an ancient temple in Ephesus, Turkey listening to the story of the life of Mary Magdalene, or Miriyam, and a soul group that was incarnated upon Earth 2000 years ago.

Mary made no mention of the format in which I had chosen to write the book. She was focused on getting her message out, a message woven throughout the pages of this book. I felt immense love and gratitude from her on how I had chosen to present her words.

A person in the publishing industry asked me, "Why did you write this book in the way of the Ancient Oriental Teachings?"

I answered, "This story wrote itself that way. After receiving feedback on the manuscript, I knew from reading books like the *Bhagavad-Gita* that this is the way it had come through me."

Sisterhood of the Dove offers the reader the opportunity to view the world completely anew. This book evolves the reader as he or she moves through its pages. The Spirit of the Dove begins to expand the reader's consciousness as he or she moves beyond fear, jealousy, power, and control. Through this book, the reader explores what changes, if any, have happened since Mary walked the Garden, Earth, reminding him or her once again that all people are part of a new paradigm coming forth to restore the Garden.

Mary's last dictated words were, "Thank you for anchoring this energy into the planetary grid of

Earth." She smiled her gratitude and I saw that we had completed part of our soul contract together. The book had not been written; it was still on audiotape and scrapes of paper; it was a skeleton of words, but for Mary, who represents a voice of the Earth Mother, it was complete. She had passed on the energy to actualize it within the Garden.

CHAPTER 1
ADVENT

Rachel had been full of defiance upon her arrival in the city of Ephesus[1] as a young girl. She had never wanted to leave Judah[2], but her mother, Miriyam, had offered no choice.

Now, standing on the top step of the temple erected by her mother, grandmother, and others who had come before her, she felt a joy beyond words.

Rachel was in her late 40s; almost 40 harvests, which the sisters called festivals[3], had passed since her Uncle Joseph's boat had docked upon the shores of Anatolia[4]. She had grown under the watchful eye of the Goddess Isis and, 30 festivals ago, had accepted her role as the Priestess of Storytelling.

Rachel watched as the last of the women and

children entered the temple. The Servers guided them to their rightful places. It was initiation time again, an event which happened once a festival. Her heart filled with the love of the Goddess and she was reminded of the master plan for which she had volunteered. "Thank you," came from her lips as she descended the temple stairs, walked across the grass, and came to the area she had prepared to tell the story. Reaching the table, she picked up the chimes her mother had given her at the time of her sacred union with Daniel, and shook them gently. The soft, tinkling sound quieted the women, who in turn brought their children to silence.

Rachel saw over 400 women and children seated upon the ground before her. She laughed and waved back to a young boy who waved to her. She began to speak.

"Early afternoons will be for resting. These rest times are most important, as we prepare you in your dreams for these evening gatherings.

"My story will focus on a soul group of 22[5]. Many of you have heard of the people within this soul group; others here do not know of them in a conscious way. It is not important at this time that you are intimately aware of each, yet I shall invoke each being's name, for as you know, or as you will learn, to invoke the name of another brings their energy to you. This is why we teach you to think several times before calling forth a person's name. The 22 are: Elizabeth and Zechariah, mother and father of the one whom many called John the

SISTERHOOD OF THE DOVE

Baptist; Mary, mother of Yeshua, and my grandmother; Joseph, uncle of Yeshua from Arimathea; John, cousin of Yeshua, whom many also called The Baptist; Yeshua, son of Mary and Joseph of Bethlehem, and my father; Miriyam, wife of Yeshua, and my mother; James, son of Mary, and my uncle; Sarah, first daughter of Yeshua and Miriyam, and my sister; Andrew and Bartholomew, the brothers James and John; Judas, Matthew, Philip, Simon of Canaan, and Peter, who changed his name to Simon Peter; and also Thaddeus and Thomas. Each of these men, along with my uncle James, traveled with Yeshua and considered themselves *brothers*.

"That leaves two more, of whom I am one: Rachel, second daughter of Yeshua and Miriyam; and a Roman named Saul who changed his name to Paul; he would later fill the void left by Yeshua's cousin Judas, after his departure.

"This story also has a small focus on 12 highly evolved beings who came to act as the gate openers for the teachings that the 22 would pass on. These beings allowed themselves to be called Magi.

"Mostly however, this story will focus on one particular being: my mother, Miriyam. Her inspiration is what brings us all here. Her love of the Goddess, her commitment to carrying out her part of the soul contract, and her journey through life is the foundation of this temple's teaching. Everything in her life became her initiation into the embodiment of the dove."

Rachel paused for a moment and raised her cup of water to her lips. She drank slowly; giving herself time to prepare the words she would say next. A young woman of 15 raised her hand.

"Yes, dear?" Rachel responded.

Boldly, the young woman asked, "Is your mother still alive?"

"Yes," Rachel answered, and readied herself to begin the next part of her story.

"Listen now, children, as our adventure begins.

"The being that would become Miriyam whispered the name she desired into her mother's ear before she was born. Her mother granted the request. The name Miriyam has a few meanings, one of which is, *sea of bitterness*. Miriyam chose this name to awaken people and remind them of the symbolic bitter waters within their emotional bodies.

"Miriyam birthed herself into the town of Migdal, in Judah, during early spring. Her mother was a quiet, beautiful woman who did what she must for her husband and three children. For the most part, however, her mother was unhappy. She had married a much older man, as she came from a poor family and her parents wanted someone to provide for her. Her husband, who had financial status, treated her as someone beneath him. He often berated her, and was unkind to his family.

"Miriyam was born the middle child, with an older brother and a younger sister. In her youth, she was intelligent and beautiful, and many women were jealous of her. She was not a quiet child, and, unlike her mother and brother, often fought with her father. When he spoke to her mother in an unkind way, Miriyam would say to him, 'The Talmud and the teachings of the Torah say you must respect your wife, and honor her. What you are doing is not right.' She was strong-minded and stood for truth, often upset by the injustices of life.

"Miriyam attended women's schooling in the traditional, communal way and learned the teachings of the Torah. She was prepared to keep a kosher home as a traditional Jewish wife and mother. One of the things she learned during this time was embroidery; it was a meditation for her, and she embroidered often with my grandmother, Mary, while I was growing up.

"When Miriyam was in her mid-teens, one of her uncles raped her. He was a Rabbi and a powerful teacher in their community. Her mother believed Miriyam when she said that she had been raped. Her father, however, did not, thinking that one of his brothers, a respected member of the community, would not have done this to his daughter. He threw Miriyam out of his house, calling her a whore because she was pregnant.

"Miriyam had no choice but to leave her home. Not one in her family stood by her side. She watched as her father tore his clothes[6] and yelled at her, saying, 'You are not my daughter. I will mourn the death of my daughter. I will sit seven suns.'

"When Miriyam left her family, she had no idea

where she would go or what she would do. It would be the last time Miriyam would ever see her parents or siblings.

"Imagine Miriyam, no older than some of you here, feeling unwanted, sitting on the side of the road, pregnant, crying, and not knowing what to do. She had with her a small sack of olives, cheese, bread, and dates that her mother had packed for her. It was late afternoon when a Roman litter[7] carried by slaves came up beside her with a woman in it, who saw that Miriyam was troubled and asked her what she was doing on the side of the road. Now you know how the female Jews were not allowed to speak with the Romans. Yes?" Rachel watched as the listeners nodded their heads.

"Miriyam, always outspoken, said to her, 'I was thrown out of my house.' The Roman woman asked her if she was good with cleaning, and Miriyam told her it was so. The Roman woman invited Miriyam to join her household.

"The Roman woman liked Miriyam, and, though she was jealous of Miriyam's beauty, she knew that Miriyam was pregnant and did not have the heart to ask her to leave. Miriyam was also very loving toward the woman's children.

"The time came for Miriyam to give birth. During the birthing process, Miriyam lost consciousness and while out of her body two things happened; in this dimension, she had twins. Her first-born, a girl, was born breech and the midwives thought her dead. They wrapped the baby and prepared it for a funeral. Her second-born was a son.

"While out of body Miriyam also met with her counterpart in the over-soul group. I previously named each of the soul group of 22. Now I want you to expand your view. The complete soul group is one of 44. Twenty-two were incarnated in the Garden[8] and 22 remained in Spirit, each connected to and responsible for guiding the incarnated ones to fulfill their contract." Rachel looked around to see if the listeners were with her before she continued.

"Miriyam had visitations with her counterpart throughout her life and knew that she was not alone. The over-soul recommended she keep her son, and when the time came, she was to leave the house of the Roman woman with him. Miriyam also received the message to nurse her son, and under no circumstances was she to allow the Roman woman to take him away from her.

"When Miriyam came to, she was presented with her son and not told that her other child had died. A short time after giving birth, the Roman woman came to her saying, 'If you want to keep your son you may stay here no longer; you will have to leave.'

"Following the guidance of her over-soul, Miriyam prepared to move. She was led to a colony of lepers located on the outskirts of Jerusalem, in the direction of Jericho, where she moved with her son, Baruch. Feeling connected with her over-soul, Miriyam felt no physical harm would come to Baruch and her.

"Now she had to find new work. Walking toward Jerusalem, she came upon a brothel. Thinking to herself, 'I have a child to take care of,' she entered the brothel and asked the madam if she had any work available. Seeing her beauty and knowing she would attract business, the madam offered Miriyam a position as a *working girl*. Miriyam knew that she was not to make money in this way and as she began to leave, a feeling came over the madam. She was deeply touched and told Miriyam that she would find work for her cleaning the brothel instead.

"It did not take long for the madam to notice how people were drawn to Miriyam; business picked up whenever Miriyam was around and because of this the madam promoted her from her position as maid. Miriyam's new task was to serve the tea and lemonade, the fruits and foods, and to talk with the guests while they were waiting. During this time Miriyam learned from the customers to write and speak different languages, despite the fact that the language she had grown to prefer was that of silence.

"Not a sun rose or set when the madam did not attempt to change Miriyam's mind about *servicing* the men in the brothel, but Miriyam would not be moved. The madam loved Miriyam's voice and instead added singing to her task. Miriyam was paid exceptionally well.

"After Miriyam had lived in the leper community for some time, she was adopted by one of the leper families, who took particularly good care of Baruch while she worked. She in turn took care of the family by bringing them food and nursing them. From Sunday to Friday, Miriyam stayed in a room at the brothel and on Fridays returned to the community to be with Baruch, who was by this time a toddler, though he was still not speaking. Miriyam knew something was wrong with his development but this did not stop her from loving him.

"One Friday while walking back from the brothel, Miriyam, wearing a beautiful red dress the madam had given her, was confronted by an angry mob of people. They were upset at her for being inappropriately dressed on Shabbat. They ran after her, throwing stones and calling her names.

"Before long, however, a man walking with two other men came to her rescue. As the angry mob dispersed, he looked deep into her eyes and her heart melted as she thought, 'At last, I am not alone anymore.' Tears welled up in her eyes, as she knew the hardships of being on her own, the hardships of being in hiding, and the hardships of not having a family were over. In that moment, Miriyam aligned even more with her over-soul counterpart and recognized who this man was to her.

"He introduced himself as Yeshua. He was in his early 20s, simply dressed with brown hair that had a reddish tinge. He and his companions were returning to the Qumran/En-gedi area and the Essene community.

"'Where are you going?' he asked.

"'I am returning to my son,' she replied softly.

"'Please, come with me,' Yeshua encouraged. As they reached the fork in the road, Yeshua saw that Miriyam was headed in the direction of Jericho. 'Are you going to the leper community?'

"'Yes,' she answered him.

"In that moment, Yeshua was prompted to go with her; he desired to make sure she was safe, but even more, he had recognized who she was to him, as well.

"As Miriyam, Yeshua, and his two companions came down the hill into the leper community, Baruch stood, as he usually did on Friday, facing the hill, and waited for his mother. This time, for the first time ever, Baruch began running toward her, calling out, 'Ima! Ima[9]!' Miriyam did not believe it; he had never uttered a single word. Miriyam instinctively knew that the change in Baruch had come with the presence of Yeshua. She was also keenly aware that whatever felt broken inside of herself, whatever aspect of her that had lost its voice and was being mirrored back to her by Baruch's silence, had come back to life. As her son received healing on the outside, she received it on the inside.

"That evening, during the Shabbat dinner, Yeshua and his companions sat with the community eating and conversing. Near the end of the evening, Yeshua turned toward Miriyam and said, 'We will be leaving tomorrow and I would like you to join us. Will you come with us?'

"Miriyam looked away slightly and said, 'I shall consider it. I shall let you know in the morning before your departure.'

"In the morning, Miriyam told Yeshua that she would join him. She had been up all night remembering this *homecoming* feeling. As she allowed this feeling to deepen, her love for Yeshua was revealed. As her adopted family agreed to keep Baruch, even more strength filled Miriyam, solidifying her choice to follow her heart. The final confirmation came as she handed Baruch over. He had a peace about him that she had never seen before.

"Miriyam was unsure of where her life was going and where she would end up living. Her plan was to visit the Essene community with Yeshua, to see if it would suit her and Baruch, and to return to the Essene community with him if it did.

"She, Yeshua, and his two companions walked to the Salt Sea[10], Qumran/En-gedi area, and joined the Essene community. During her first few suns, she witnessed how much the community respected and loved Yeshua.

"Yeshua introduced her to his Uncle Joseph, who came from Arimathea, when he came over for a visit. Upon meeting Joseph, she knew again, 'I am not alone,' and she felt a tremendous sense of homecoming. This would happen each time Miriyam met someone from the soul group.

"During that visit, Joseph told Yeshua it was

time for them to travel again. Yeshua in turn told Miriyam that he had to leave. He told her that he would return on the next full moon and that when he returned he would introduce her to his mother and his family.

"Miriyam stayed with the Essene community for a few suns after Yeshua left. During that time, she realized she would not return to the brothel.

"Miriyam made friends with the Essenes. Among them was a maternal woman in her 40s, named Leah. Miriyam felt safe with her, as well as with the little girl who was Leah's constant companion. This child seemed familiar to Miriyam. One afternoon Miriyam asked Leah, 'Is she your grandchild?'

"Leah said, 'No, I found this child.'

"'What do you mean?'

"Leah told Miriyam that, two harvests ago, she had gone to the market in Jerusalem where she heard the sound of a baby crying. Upon locating the sound, she found the tiny girl, wrapped in fabric and ready for burial, placed on the ground. The fabric moved as she picked up the child, and, looking around, she was prompted to take the child. Being Essene, she trusted her feelings and followed her intuition. Leah finished the story, saying to Miriyam, 'I was told that when the time was right her mother would come for her.'

"At that moment Miriyam found herself crying and whispered, 'I thought my other child was dead.'

"Leah hugged her and gently said, 'No, this is

your daughter.' Leah never named the girl, believing that her mother would name her when she came for her.

"Miriyam named her daughter Rivka, and quickly returned with her to the leper community.

"The joy Miriyam felt as she reunited Baruch and Rivka was equaled only by how happy they were to see each other. It was as though their souls remembered each other and from that time on the two were inseparable. Once Baruch met Rivka, his mind healed and he became like any other young child.

"A few more suns passed and Miriyam packed her things, said good-bye to her adopted family, and took Baruch and Rivka, sleeping in a tent along the way, back to the Essene community."

Rachel took a deep breath and looked around at the sisters' faces. Some were wide-awake and others were sleeping. Rachel leaned forward, light emanated from all around her, and she felt the Goddess Isis caress her hair. She continued, "For those of you who have been in love, I ask you to recall that feeling: how your heart longed and burned with desire, how you lost much of your reason. Remember this longing. Miriyam's heart burned; it had been set ablaze by the spirit of Yeshua. Yeshua consumed her thoughts. She was in love."

Rachel beamed as she recalled the depth of the love her mother and father had shared. "My desire is for you to rest in this space of longing. This concludes the first part of our story. Rest well, recall your dreams, and eat light. Communicating your dreams is required during the morning gatherings. We shall meet in this spot when the evening twilight has come again. I ask you to exit the temple through the Ankh – the key to eternal life – and the Gateway of the North. RA BA RA."

The group rose and made its way out of the temple through the Northern Gate. Rachel was the last to leave. Later, down near the river, she gathered with the 12 Servers who were assisting her. As they sat, 100s of tents gave off a soft glow while gentle lullabies filled the air as children were lulled to sleep.

Rachel instructed the Servers on the following suns' events, saying, "During each of the next eight mornings some initiates will be sent into nature; each will go forth with prayer into the elements to greet the Sun God, Ra, in their own way. They will then proceed, with assistance from an elder, to gather different herbs for the ceremonies and for the healing of people that come to us for care.

"Some initiates will learn of the different healing herbs. They will learn how to cook and prepare them for storage, which ones to use for child birth, which ones to use as medicine for stopping pregnancy, which ones to use to create more milk for nursing mothers; and the different herb teas for babies.

"They will learn the different Goddess ways of healing the physical, mental, and emotional levels

SISTERHOOD OF THE DOVE

of people. In this way, we as the Sisterhood work
with the Land God Geb, and with the different
elements.

"Other teachings of our Sisterhood involve
astronomy: the study of objects and matter outside
the Garden's atmosphere. Here our Sisterhood
works with the Sky Goddess, Nut.

"The teachings provide each initiate with the
opportunity to excel in her own natural gifts. Each
sister is required to become proficient in all aspects
of The Teachings of the Dove.

"These next few suns for the initiates will be a
taste of the teachings they may spend a lifetime
learning."

Upon completion, each Server moved to where
she would sleep and bed down for the night. Rachel
walked down to the river, disrobed, and placed
herself gently in the moving water. As she lay there,
looking up at Nut's starry blanket, her heart filled
with awe and wonder at the magnificence of the
Goddess. As her being merged with the elements,
the thoughts of doubt she had collected from the
sisters that evening, were washed away.

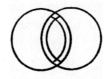

CHAPTER 2
SACRED UNION

Rachel placed the flowers she had brought upon the little table beside her seat and with a silent prayer asked Isis to spread their delicate scent throughout the temple. Her mother had always loved roses, and seeing them upon the table brought back fond memories of her.

"Aren't the flowers beautiful?" she asked the collective. "I trust you are taking time to partake in the Garden's fragrance. Let not the precious miracles of life pass you by."

Looking at a small child in front of her she asked, "How do you feel?" The child buried herself under her mother's arm while Rachel turned abruptly to her left and scanned the crowd. Looking toward its middle she focused in on an elderly woman. Once their eyes connected, Rachel rose and began to move through the sisters. As she reached the woman, Rachel knelt in front of her and whispered, "Your name: what is your name?"

"Lily."

"How does your chest feel, Lily?"

"It's sore," she replied.

Rachel stood and motioned for one of the Servers. As the Server arrived at Lily's side Rachel said, "The fire of love burns through her from last night's infusion of energy. Her body is embracing Isis faster than it can take. We need to cool the Flame of the Goddess within her. Bring her to the pool and let her drink." The Server left with Lily as Rachel returned to her seat.

Speaking to the sisters Rachel said, "Lily recalled the burning fire that Miriyam felt for Yeshua. That fire burns through her at a pace, which puts much stress on her physical body. The Goddess watches us all… takes care of us all. Remember this. The Goddess appears in every form. Look for her; call her forth; and she will bless your path."

Rachel picked up her cup, drank, and continued, "Do you recall where we were in the story? Miriyam has returned to the Essene community and is awaiting the full moon and Yeshua's return.

"Now before I go further: The Essenes are mystics; they study the Kabballah, take a stance of peace, and live in harmony with nature.

"Their diet consists mostly of the foods from the plant kingdom. They eat eggs and fowl, but these foods are reserved for the Festivals. Dried meats are prepared for times of travel and the rainy season when the floods come. Living near the Salt Sea, the lowest point in the Garden, they may not, at times, leave the area to reach the markets. When the floods come, the water washes out the roads.

"The Essenes believe in a system of barter, exchanging goods with different communities that surround the Qumran/En-gedi area. They do not believe in the monetary system, a system put into effect throughout the country by King Herod and the Sanhedrin: the supreme council and tribunal of the Jews.

"The Essenes live primarily in the mountains. For this reason they work with caves, creating most of their living space in caverns. However, when traveling to the Salt Sea, they use a particular style of tent as their abode.

"Now I return to Miriyam and her love.

"Miriyam waited 13 suns for Yeshua's return and when next she fixed her eyes upon him, her heart danced with elation. He entered the community with his uncle Joseph and several other unfamiliar people. Desire[11] to be with him burned throughout her body as he approached her; she barely contained herself. Yeshua introduced her to his mother, Mary, and several of his brothers and sisters. They visited while dinner was prepared, served, and eaten. Following the meal they played with the children before they were put to bed.

"As Miriyam emerged from her cave, Yeshua excused himself from the group of men he was speaking with and came over to her.

"'Will you walk with me?' he asked.

"Miriyam nodded.

"They walked together, spoke of his family, and he asked her how she was feeling. Miriyam was cautious to reveal her true feelings, although she felt he already knew.

"Yeshua asked, 'Miriyam, do you remember the *dream*?'

"'I remember a dream that words fail to describe,' she responded.

"'Do you remember *our* mission?' he asked.

"'Yes,' Miriyam answered softly, lowering her head. 'I do. We are but two of several; I recall a being, not of human form, that watches over me. I recall the energy of a fog placed upon the people for which I have no name. It is this fog that we have come to dispel. I recall the feeling of its suffocating fear. I recall, also, the opposite of this fog and fear. Each time I meet one who serves the mission, my heart feels a special warmth, my mind is cleared of the fog, and my fears melt away. It happened with your uncle Joseph and it happened with your mother and your brother James. That feeling happened with you when we first met. Unlike your mother, brother, and uncle, however, I have other feelings about you and us.'

"Yeshua, turning to her, said, 'Then your soul

recalls…' his voice faded.

"Miriyam lifted her head, looked into his eyes, and smiled.

"Yeshua said to her, 'Since we parted, I have remembered the depth of my love for you. I would be honored if… will you unite with me?'

"Miriyam's heart felt as if it would explode and she said, 'I, too, have recalled the depth of my love for you, Yeshua, and I would love nothing more.'

"Yeshua's voice changed in that moment. It was something that Miriyam would become accustomed to. The look in his eyes changed as well. He remained as loving and as soft; that did not change, but the energy about him was different and he spoke from a distant place. 'I ask you to surrender your human will to the Divine Spirit as the time for our union was set prior to our ever meeting. It takes place on the next full moon and preparations are well underway. It is for us to surrender, my love.'

"Miriyam nodded and the two walked back, mostly in silence, holding hands.

"It was not long before Joseph, Yeshua, and Miriyam were off to the ceremonial site of the union. Miriyam was led from the community during the night into the mountains where for the first time she met a group of beings, known as the Hathors, who were making their home on what we call the Morning Star[12]. For those of you unfamiliar with the Morning Star, it is that bright, shining light to the East. The Hathors welcomed her by name, as if they had known her forever, and urged all three to enter their flying ship.

"The Hathors informed her that they were flying to a place called Alba[13]." Rachel paused to observe the sisters' faces when presented the idea of a flying ship and beings from a distant world. She saw excitement, disbelief, recognition, doubt, eagerness, and nervousness.

"Imagine this," she continued, "Miriyam, who has never left Judah, has walked onto a ship that flies. That flying ship begins moving over the ground in a way that seems magic to her on one level and yet is familiar to her on another. She is flying to the place of her sacred union, a place she knows not. She has left Rivka and Baruch, who are still toddlers, behind, with Mary and a community she is just getting to know. Most of her life she has not trusted many with her children." Rachel took a breath and continued, "Imagine the sense of trust Miriyam must have had to do all of this. Do you understand that once she recalled a large portion of the mission, that knowing permeated her being, filling her with the trust and faith required to fulfill it?"

Rachel looked around to see how the sisters were receiving what she was saying, allowing them to recall the choice they each made before incarnating, their choice to enter the Sisterhood. They were also meant to remember that by being present in the temple during this time, they were opening to the trust and faith that would allow them to pass on the teachings, when they were called to do so.

Rachel continued, "The Hathors took them to three islands off of the mainland coast of Alba. Miriyam learned that the first island held a magnificent sacred site. She called it a stone circle[14]. These rough-cut, elongated stones, similar to our smaller pillars, stand on end in the fields placed in specific shapes and patterns.

"The second island she visited she called The Place of the Dove[15], and the third island, they called Peaked Island[16]. On the first two stops, the Hathors welcomed various men and women aboard. Yeshua told Miriyam that these people were coming to their union. When they landed on Peaked Island, all but the Hathors left the ship, and Yeshua stayed behind for a moment to arrange their return.

"On Peaked Island, Miriyam met a being who looked as no other man she had ever seen before. Every hair on her body bristled when she looked into his eyes. Yeshua informed Miriyam that the *man* was a Magus[17] and that he, along with another being that was already upon the mainland, would be performing their sacred union ceremony.

"The entire party left Peaked Island by boat, crossing the water to the mainland. They used a boat at this point because several new members of the party traveling with them were not of the vibration to travel with the Hathors.

"Let me speak of the Hathors for a moment. Think of them as your elder brothers and sisters who came from another universe by way of Sirius[18] and settled on the Morning Star. They choose to serve the Garden and her peoples in our evolution.

"While Yeshua and Miriyam walked to the place of their union, Miriyam enjoyed the countryside of a land she hardly knew. It was late in the spring and the flowers were well in bloom. Along the way, people of all ages joined their party and Miriyam was introduced to a community of people known as the Druids. They informed her that she was walking upon the sacred Line of the Rose, an energetic line which traveled around the Garden and held many healing properties which were a blessing for all who walked upon it. Miriyam would come to understand why her heart flushed upon hearing this.

"Miriyam was surprised to see how well known Yeshua was in Alba. The men, women, and children deeply honored and respected him.

"The full moon, the time of their union, was three suns hence. Miriyam had absolutely no control over how the ceremony would look. She did not choose her dress or any of the things for the ceremony. She surrendered to the wonderful Druid community that was similar in many ways to the Essene.

"Upon arriving near the location where the ceremony would take place, Miriyam was told by the Druid women that she must say good-bye to Yeshua; she was to be prepared for their sacred union and would see Yeshua again in three suns' time.

"During those three suns, Miriyam learned from these women the Goddess ways of a Druid Union. The women prepared her with song, flute music, and herbs. Miriyam listened attentively, even though she did not recognize the language, and she enjoyed the teachings on one level, but her yearning to be with Yeshua was a distraction on another.

"At the dawn of the third sun, Miriyam said her prayers and made her way to the place where she would be dressed. The Druid women presented her with an emerald green dress; the sleeves hung from her arms when she put it on; she had not worn clothing like this before. Upon her head, they placed a garland of fresh, white flowers, which the women had prepared. Around her neck, they placed a magnificent necklace; on the end of a long line of beads was a large wing made of dove feathers with a single, red rose at its center.

"It was from the Druids that Miriyam received her symbol: the same dove and rose which are on the East Arch of the temple.

"Many people have ceased to remember the Devic Kingdom, what you may call the Elementals or Fairies, since Yeshua graduated his physical form. It is important to note however that their full presence manifested as a blessing for the sacred union of Yeshua and Miriyam.

"As Ra moved high in the sky, the women formed a procession, placing Miriyam about a third of the way back.

"Miriyam's anticipation at seeing Yeshua paled

in comparison to actually seeing him as she moved past the trees and entered the clearing that was to be their sanctuary[19]. The Druid community gathered – men, women, and children – in the grassy field. To the east stood an altar upon which lay a large, heavy, metal box. Its lid was open and she saw its golden fabric lining. Standing up in the box was a metal chalice with 12 different gems surrounding its bowl. Miriyam did not recall ever seeing items such as these anywhere before. In front of the altar stood the Magus and an old, almost ancient, woman, whom Yeshua later called a Crone, to bless their union.

"Yeshua entered the clearing from the right and Miriyam entered from the left; the two made their way to the altar accompanied by gentle flute music. They took their vows in silence, sharing love and remembrance with their eyes, knowing that their communication must be beyond words.

"The Magus turned and picked up the chalice. Miriyam saw the weight of it by the effort he made to lift it. As he held the chalice in his left hand, the Crone placed her right hand upon it and the two moved it forward for Miriyam to drink. She touched the chalice only with her lips. After she had taken a sip, the Magus and the Crone brought the chalice to Yeshua, who placed his lips where Miriyam's had been, and drank.

"The Crone returned the chalice to the altar and picked up two white candles, which had been burning since the beginning of the ceremony; she handed one to the Magus. The Magus walked slowly in a counterclockwise direction, while the Crone walked slowly in a clockwise direction. They dripped wax around Miriyam and Yeshua, sealing the sacredness of their union and their destiny.

"As the Magus and the Crone dripped the wax around them, Miriyam focused upon the Crone. She saw tears rolling down her cheeks. In that moment Miriyam knew they were not tears of joy; whatever those tears meant and whatever the foreboding feelings were, Miriyam was soon to find out.

"The Magus and the Crone, after completing their circles, stood in front of the couple again. Each bowed, giving their blessings, and the people in attendance voiced their joy with music, dance, and singing.

"Miriyam and Yeshua were ushered out of the clearing toward the base of a particular oak tree in the forest. Behind the tree was an opening in the land, where Miriyam and Yeshua descended, led by two men and two women. They walked underground to a place upon the Rose Line prepared specifically for them. After Miriyam and Yeshua settled, the two men and two women left.

"It was here that my sister Sarah was conceived, that evening beneath the Garden.

"In the middle of the night, Miriyam and Yeshua returned to the surface, and, as they made their way back to the clearing, they came upon the Magus and the Crone, who had with them the metal box. Miriyam wondered if she would ever see that magnificent chalice again. As they moved on, Yeshua told her that the Magus and the Crone were taking the chalice to the opening in the Rose Line, where it was to be left with the entrance sealed. He went on to say that, if their mission went as desired, then the soul group of 22 would anchor the vibration of unconditional love upon the Garden and the chalice would be returned to the Holy Temple in Jerusalem[20]. For now, however, the chalice would stay in Alba, which was the geographic Heart of the Goddess and under the care of the Druid Guardians, the Hathors, and some others who were not of human frequency.

"When she and Yeshua entered the clearing, Miriyam became aware of the large celebration that had been prepared in honor of their love. She was full of gratitude for what the Druid men and women had done; Miriyam had never imagined a union and a celebration so beautiful.

"That night during the celebration, Miriyam connected with three women near her age--late teens--who would remain her friends for life. These three women dedicated their lives to nature and the Goddess and made the choice not to marry, not to have children. Later, each became learned in midwifery, medicine, and herbs. These women became part of the Sisterhood and joined Miriyam when she moved to Gaul[21] in the later part of her life.

"A few suns after their sacred union, Yeshua informed Miriyam that they would be traveling throughout Alba with several people from the Druid community, connecting with and talking to different peoples and owners of land. Yeshua told her that he had arranged for the Hathors to pick them up on Peaked Island in about a moon and a half. The purpose for their travel was to create different centers for people to commune in, and to invoke the unity of the Druid and Essene communities. They were also to teach, and raise the consciousness of the peoples of Alba who did not belong to the Druid community.

"The moon phases passed and they made their way back to Peaked Island. Joseph, Yeshua, and Miriyam greeted the Hathors and returned to the Essene community.

"At the time of the Sirius Alignment[22], they returned to the Essene community. Yeshua wanted to be back with his mother, Mary, and his community to celebrate.

"Upon their return, the community had a large celebration honoring Sirius, the Goddess celebration, and the sacred union of Miriyam and Yeshua.

"The community held few secrets and Mary took on informing Rivka and Baruch of their mother's union with Yeshua.

"The Druid women confided in Miriyam that she had conceived upon the consummation of their union and that she and Yeshua were to have a girl child.

"Miriyam was happy to see Rivka and Baruch and told them that they were going to have a younger sister.

"The time of pregnancy for Miriyam was challenging. She was instructed not go anywhere on her own. She was to ask for assistance from the community for almost everything. This made her uncomfortable, as she was an independent person. It was a grand exercise in surrender and allowing others to support her. But, Miriyam was not allowed to travel with Yeshua, to which she had become accustomed, and she loved traveling. This pregnancy felt confining and the Essene community seemed imprisoning. But the health of Miriyam's unborn child depended upon it."

Rachel reached over, picked up the flowers, and invited one of the younger children to come forward. The child approached and Rachel handed her the flowers. As the child returned to her seat Rachel spoke, "As Miriyam was guided to remain still to nurture the gift of love in her womb, I, too, advise you this evening to be still and allow the love of Isis to grow within you. This brings the second part of our story to completion. We are serving tea tonight; please drink of the herbs, rest, and before you know it, we shall sit together again. Please follow the Servers, as they will direct you to exit the temple through the Gateway of the North East and the symbol of the Vesica Pisces. The Vesica Pisces symbolizes perfect love, sacred union, and ultimate surrender between two souls in human form. Made of two interlocking rings, the edge of each ring touches the center of the other. The message of the

Vesica Pisces is that to fully embrace the heart of your beloved, you must be willing to allow him to fully embrace your heart at the exact same moment. RA BA RA."

The temple cleared and Rachel stretched out upon the grass, drinking in the energy of the land through her spine to rejuvenate herself. She smiled as she recalled her mother's voice speaking of her union with her father. This lesson of union carried on in Rachel's life with everyone and everything. It was the teaching of true intimacy; being united with her husband, Daniel, her children, and her grandchildren brought forth constant teachings of the Vesica Pisces. The teachings did not stop with family. Her acceptance of sitting in the Seat of the Temple offered her the opportunity, each sun, to embrace all beings with whom she connected and allow them into her center as she moved into theirs. "The Goddess has designed it well," she thought. She rose and headed toward the North East Gate, offering thanks in the direction of Isis.

CHAPTER 3
THE MAKING OF A PRIESTESS

Miriyam spent the rest time of the afternoon in meditation, as she had the previous two suns, and would continue for each sun of the storytelling. She sat with the collective higher self of the group at the temple and instructed them in the art of breathing.

Coming out of meditation, Rachel looked around the temple. Eight arches stood tall, each with symbols carved into them. Rachel finished breathing in each of the symbols, and expanded her awareness in appreciation outward past the temple to the temple grounds. Further away were simple houses and buildings, used for living, storage, teaching, healing, and all things a community required; some were made of stone and mortar, others of mud and straw.

The males in the community had a house for prayer and worship. This house was open to females. The temple, however, was open only to females and boys under the age of 13 when accompanied by their mothers, and was for teaching the ways of the Goddess.

At the age of three, the young boys entered their own school within the community. Upon reaching 13, these young men went to learn the ways of the active principle. When the boys were ready to take on manhood, the women would teach them the arts of lovemaking and the different ways of honoring the female.

The community had a healing center in which various ailments of the physical, mental, and emotional were addressed, as well as numerous types of gardens throughout the temple grounds; in one of these gardens, the sisters grew an assortment of herbs. The herb garden was unique, in that it held seeds from all over the world. Seeds were brought to the area in various ways, one of which was Rachel's Uncle Joseph of Arimathea, a businessman who operated several boats and made his rounds throughout the Great Sea[23] as a merchant.

Males were restricted from the temple as they were not to awaken their energy in a sexual way. If a man were to be in the temple, and create a sense of passion and lust, then it would compromise the energy of the entire temple. In support of this, women would wear clothing that would cover them. The intent was to create a *lust* for spirit, instead of a lust for the flesh. People focused on spirit, instead of temptation.

Rachel rose and headed off to enjoy a meal. During mealtime, she asked the Servers to make sure each of the sisters was told to bring warm clothing or a blanket for the evening storytelling.

* * * * *

As the Goddess had transmitted to her, the temperature had dropped significantly that evening. Rachel had concern for the young ones. She herself had put on two sweaters and was wearing her shawl.

"Do any of you need more blankets? The Servers will get you some if you do."

Rachel raised her left arm and formed the dove call sounds taught to her by her grandmother. Three doves responded. Two landed upon the backrest of her seat, one on either side of her head, and the third on her left wrist. She brought her left hand to her lap and while petting the dove gently with the other, spoke, "Do you recall what happened to Lily yesterday? She has served each one of us here. As you will learn, we are all connected. What happens to one of us, happens to all of us. As we grow in unity and release the veils of separation, we come to know that when one cries, we all cry; when one rejoices, we all rejoice, and, as in the case of this dove here, by warming one, the Goddess warms us all. These doves have responded to the call of the Goddess, as did Miriyam and Yeshua.

"Miriyam learned to surrender her personal will to that of the Divine Will. The Essenes were not in the habit of welcoming people into their community. Usually, new people entered the community with an existing member, and in Miriyam's case, it was no different. She entered the community through Yeshua, and the Essenes embraced her as one their own, showing her the same respect they held for Yeshua. She once said it this way to me. 'If he were a king, they treated me as a queen.' This made Miriyam feel uncomfortable. She was one who enjoyed her privacy and now privacy was almost non-existent. She used to enjoy walking down from the mountain toward the Salt Sea alone. Now that she was with child, however, each time people from the community saw her leave, they would appear around her, saying, 'We shall not let you go alone.' The community was worried for her because she was not strong.

"As for Rivka and Baruch, who were barely over age three, they stayed mostly with Mary, their aunts, their uncles, and their cousins. My grandmother chose never to unite with a man after her husband, Joseph, died. Rivka, who had been in the community all but a few moments of her life with Baruch as her inseparable companion, thrived in the community environment. Baruch studied with the Rabbis, learning the traditional ways of the Essene, and Rivka studied with the women. The children spent the Holy Sabbath with Miriyam and Yeshua and the rest of the family.

"Yeshua was led to travel a lot and was constantly coming and going. Miriyam traveled with him during the times she was not pregnant. Yeshua was fulfilling his part of the soul contract by accepting his training and offering teachings. Upon each return, he would speak with Miriyam about his adventures. She loved the stories he told of the peoples in the Garden. Miriyam especially loved the stories of his meetings with the Magi. Yeshua told her that the plan was for him to meet with 12 Magi, many in different parts of the world.

"The love of Miriyam and Yeshua for each other manifested on several different levels. Theirs was a human love as well as a divine love. Many of the levels upon which their love manifested do not exist in this world. Yeshua and Miriyam would often meet on the inner worlds.

"When Yeshua would travel, Miriyam missed him deeply. They had the power to travel in the dreamtime and even though he was not always present physically, it was never as if he was not there on some level. They used this gift often and connected frequently.

"Each time Yeshua returned from a meeting with a Magus, he returned with another DNA strand connected. As Miriyam merged with Yeshua upon his return, she too was reconnecting the strands of

DNA within herself, all the while evolving as the equal of Yeshua."

Rachel paused and contemplated what to say next. "Once Miriyam met Yeshua, the constant visitations of the over-soul began to lessen considerably. This was because her strands of DNA had begun to reconnect at that point.

"Now, I mentioned a few moments ago that Miriyam and Yeshua would connect on the inner worlds. They left this reality for what seemed like moments and would be in another reality for what seemed a cycle of the moon. During the times Yeshua was traveling, they would leave their bodies and connect. Miriyam received many messages from Yeshua, some of which she told to Mary and the rest of the community.

"Miriyam and Yeshua were living with Mary, when Mary began to teach Miriyam the ways of the Goddess. Mary was the mother Miriyam never had and they loved each other deeply. Miriyam learned that Mary, in her youth, had gone to the mouth of the Aur River[24] in Egypt and studied the ways of the Goddess in the Temple of Isis. Mary explained that during the moment of the physical conception of Yeshua she also conceived the energy of the Goddess within her womb. Mary went on to say that Miriyam's child, my older sister Sarah, would be the one to continue the Goddess consciousness. Her part of the soul contract called for her to remain celibate. She would choose to travel with the Goddess energy, and serve as her father was serving, in the sense that her father moved through life with the Goddess consciousness.

"Throughout the time of Miriyam's pregnancy, part of her teachings from Mary involved the healing of all of her lessons of abuse. Mary told her that if she was to embody the consciousness of the Goddess, then it was vital for her to forgive and accept her past.

"Mary taught Miriyam about the various herbs and plants, and how to prepare them and take them. She taught her how to speak to the Garden, and how to lie upon her and send healing energies from one location to another. Mary taught her how to commune with the Devic Realm and work with the power of manifestation that the Elementals[25] offered.

"They frequented the Salt Sea and Miriyam became learned in the art of purifying the body of negative energies, examples of which are fear, illness, or energy that does not resonate with love. Miriyam learned to commune with the Thunder Beings[26] and learned how to call the rains forth; she would stand in the rain to clear herself of negative energies. She learned how to use all of the elements of nature to aid her. She would be with the trees and ask them to listen to her tears. The trees would listen to her cries to the Goddess. Miriyam healed the residue of abuse within herself and found self-acceptance."

Rachel stopped and leaned forward, "This is extremely important. Do you understand that there are no victims? All experiences are for us to grow and learn. Miriyam endured each hardship because, as I mentioned earlier, when one heals, we *all* heal. It is as if one threw a stone into a pond. The ripples formed from this action will touch all shores. Let it equally be said that Miriyam also chose each grace within her life.

"By the time her third child was born Miriyam held no resentment or anger towards any of the beings that she had allowed to injure her. She forgave herself and was full of gratitude towards each soul who had served her while in this Garden. Miriyam had not yet healed the lessons of fear, however.

"The time came for the birth of my sister, and, as usual, the women of the community prepared a sacred birthing space, with midwives present, women to fetch water, women to fetch herbs. The smells of lavender and peppermint hung in the air. Song and prayer filled the cave as my sister came forth into the world. Miriyam was fed fennel seed tea to give her milk a rich quality and to make it flow with ease. During the sun following the birth, Miriyam was kept still and fed mostly liquids: teas, juices, and water, to rid her body of poisons. After a time, fruits were given to increase the sweetness of her milk, and, if she desired, then cheeses and goat's milk were available.

"After the completion of a sun, Yeshua was allowed to enter the sacred space and Miriyam introduced him to their daughter. As you know, it is tradition for the mother to name her children and Miriyam chose that of their daughter, Sarah.

"Sarah was beautiful and born with a full head of hair. Her skin was light in color and her eyes were light gray, deep eyes in which one becomes lost. Sarah, as one of the soul group, was born with full memory of the 22 and their soul contract. She was a content child, sensitive to everything around her. She loved to play with Miriyam's long, chestnut brown hair as she rode upon her back. Miriyam always wore her hair up in a braid when she was outside her abode, and Sarah loved to play with it and pull out her braid with her long, thin fingers.

"Sarah learned to speak early; about eight moons had passed, and when she began to speak it was in a tongue Miriyam did not understand. Yeshua understood Sarah, however, and had conversations with her in this foreign tongue. When Miriyam heard Yeshua and Sarah talking, she asked him what language they were speaking and Yeshua looked up, smiled at her, and said, 'Not from this planet.'

"One of the greatest teachings Miriyam received from Yeshua was taught through Sarah's behavior. When Sarah was about a festival old, she crawled away and out of Miriyam's sight. Miriyam became frantic over her disappearance and went for Yeshua.

"Yeshua yelled, jolting her into a centered state, exclaiming, 'Be not attached to the fruit of your womb. To the same extent that you love your children, you will love everyone else. The child has her spirit, and she has her protectors.'

"At that point, Miriyam retorted, 'Why do I have all these people following me around when I want my privacy?' He laughed and walked away.

"After Yeshua had walked away, Miriyam knew, 'There is nothing I can control. There is nothing I should want to control. I need only fall into the arms of the Goddess and trust.' As she surrendered to this knowing, a dark cloud came up and out from the base of her spine through her heart. Miriyam physically saw gray smoke emerge from her body and leave her being. She felt different after that. She looked into one of her shiny, metal plates and saw that she had changed.

"It was during the next sun that Yeshua looked at Miriyam with his beautiful smile and gave her the most tender hug. Miriyam wept in his arms while he petted her head. He never told her he was proud of her, in words, but he radiated it and she felt it to the depths of her being.

"Yeshua knew she had released the dark cloud, as it was he who had assisted her in weaving another one of her DNA strands together. Yeshua had at this point met with 10 of the 12 Magi. As he held her she began crying and he softly whispered, 'From this moment forth you are my equal.'

"Do you recall that Miriyam had not healed her lessons of fear? With the release of that dark cloud, Miriyam released the last remnants of fear from her being. She often joked that if Yeshua had not assisted her, then she would have gone mad, because Sarah was an adventurous child who did a lot of teleportation. Often none knew where she was. Mary once said of Sarah's disappearances, 'Fret not, she is with the Hathors; do not worry, for she has gone to study and learn.'

"Sarah spent much of her time in the elements and with the Devic Kingdom. Sarah spoke less and less as she grew older, but when she did, her words carried weight, and she was extremely gifted when it came to learning languages. Miriyam knew languages, but not the way Sarah did. It did not take much to spark her knowledge. She also excelled in arithmetic and was of great help to Uncle Joseph when she became older, as he used her ability to calculate travel and goods. Sarah did travel with him to Alba when the Goddess called her to leave.

"It was upon that sun, after Miriyam accepted herself as Yeshua's equal, that he and she consummated their relationship in a deeply tender way, and I was conceived. She shared with me that in the cells of her body, she increasingly embraced the consciousness of knowing.

"Miriyam began radiating this consciousness all the time. She was clear of mind and heart, and, when she spoke, people absorbed her words as the desert absorbs the rain. They would not question her; the people held no doubt. Miriyam experienced a complete alignment with her over-soul. This alignment granted her the ability to teleport."

Rachel paused at this point during the story,

picked up her flowers, and smelled them. She had always been shy and never enjoyed when the attention was placed directly upon her. The next part of the story always offered her an opportunity to express true humility[27].

Rachel took a long, slow breath and resumed, "They tell me I came early, right in the middle of the Pesach ceremony[28]. They were not anticipating me until after Pesach. Miriyam always believed that because I was born at this time, I gravitated to all forms of ceremonies.

"I am two festivals younger than my sister Sarah. I was an extremely fussy child who complained a lot. I, unlike Sarah when she was young, wanted Father around. His frequent absences left a void inside me. I used to wonder where he went, and, when I asked, the answer I received never felt right. People said, 'Your father has gone, by ship, to Gaul and Spain and other places, with Uncle Joseph.' I wanted more. Looking back, however, I realize that no answer would have been enough because I wanted him home and near me.

"My behavior around missing Father changed when I was three; our family had another child at that time and it seemed that whatever was maternal in me came to life. I loved taking care of my younger brother, Binyamin. I was protective over him and loved him dearly. I would watch over him when Mother went to collect the water and do the errands. I have always loved to sing, and, while Binyamin was young, I would sing him to sleep.

"Mother told me that the healing she experienced upon the sun of my conception was what allowed me to join in sacred union with a man, have children, hold the energy of the Goddess, and continue the lineage of our family.

"She said that Sarah had come forth with an entirely different mission from mine: a life of abstinence and serving the Goddess.

"Miriyam was in her early 20s when Binyamin was born. Father had been away for a long time; I was told that his travel this time would take him about 18 moons. I did not know how long that was, but it was a long time. Binyamin's was the only birth that took place while Father was away.

"Shortly after Binyamin was born the women noticed that he had a problem in the upper palate area of his mouth. He did not suckle at our mother's breast; he did not drink her milk.

"Mother's heart hurt, as she felt that, when it came to making sons, she always did something wrong, since both her sons were born with physical imperfections."

Rachel rested for a moment. Then asked, "Do you sense how on one level Miriyam is balanced, and then in a moment, her humanness comes to the fore, causing her great suffering?"

The mothers among the listeners nodded, and Rachel resumed her story. "The women worked with Binyamin using herbs and slowly, the palate began to mend. They made a dropper out of fabric to feed him the milk.

"Sarah and I began speaking much earlier than Binyamin did; he had a temper, and he was smart, but according to Miriyam, we were all smart. Miriyam and Yeshua had no favorites in our family. Each of us was encouraged to manifest our own unique inner gifts which the Goddess had given us.

"During the 18 moons that Father was traveling, unbeknownst to us, Miriyam had a series of disturbing visions. She consulted a Rabbi within the community. Out of compassion and protection for Mary, Miriyam chose not to speak of her visions involving Yeshua. She trusted that the Rabbi would give intellectual understanding to these visions.

"Miriyam missed Yeshua during these 18 moons and would go off and speak with him on the inner world. She taught us how to do this. She said to me, 'I know he feels me. I know he hears me. All I have to do is talk with him. All you have to do is talk with him.' When I was older, I asked her about those times and she told me, 'When your father is not around I feel a physical void, but I do not feel an energetic void.'

"At times, none of us reached him, not even Miriyam. These were the times when he was going through his special training. But even during these times, when it got difficult for Miriyam, she would dream of him or connect some other way.

"I was told of the visions only when I was much older after they actually came true. The Goddess was preparing me to sit in this seat, and, although reluctant, Miriyam saw the value in telling me, as she knew I would be telling you at some point.

"She reminded me of the bad winter back then. It was after the time of paying taxes and after Rosh Hashanah—the New Year. It had been raining hard and she had been holding and looking at Binyamin, her heart breaking because he did not suckle. As she sat trying to feed him, he fell asleep; this is when the Goddess gave her a vision of the times to come. More visions would follow shortly after. Miriyam saw that she would not be with Yeshua forever and that a group of men would take him from her. The Goddess gave her only partial details of how this would occur, but she did see great challenges for the soul group of 22, and for the people of her country. She saw that she would physically lose Yeshua. I do not know if she saw more than she wanted to see, but she did see her beloved hanging from a cross, metal spikes through his wrists and feet. She also saw that she would not be in Judah. She could not imagine this; she loved Judah.

"It was extremely difficult for her to see Yeshua upon the cross because she knew that this is how people are punished and she did not know why someone gentle as Yeshua would be punished. She said that she did not understand the visions and dismissed them as symbolism because that was easier to believe.

"After the first vision was complete, her thoughts returned to the image of the Crone in tears, as she poured the wax around them upon their sacred union day to seal and acknowledge their commitment to the mission.

"In all of the times Miriyam and Yeshua connected on the inner worlds while he was away, she never spoke to him about the visions. She waited until he returned, allowing him to integrate the teachings he was learning.

"When Yeshua did return he was in his late 20s and he had met with 11 of the 12 Magi. We were all happy to have him back; the whole community was. I remember that I ran to him and he lifted me and hugged me. He sat me down and moved toward Binyamin, whom he was seeing physically for the first time. He lifted him, and, as he held him, put his hand under Binyamin's nose. When he removed his hand, everything upon Binyamin's lip was perfect. I grabbed my father around the legs and hugged him as tightly as ever. His love was so healing. I miss holding him. I love him so much."

Rachel wiped the tears from her cheeks, took a few deep breaths, and went on, "On Fridays the family came together for the Shabbat dinner and the observance of the Sabbath: Father, Mother, Grandmother Mary, my brothers and sisters, and some of my other aunts and uncles.

"Friday nights were for storytelling. We all loved storytelling. The storytellers mixed the stories of Judaism with the Goddess teachings. Miriyam and Yeshua would play with us; it was a lot of fun.

"Yeshua, on one of those nights, shared something that I currently put forth even now. He said, 'We did not come to destroy a tradition.' I later learned that he was speaking of the soul group of 22: 'We came to awaken people to transcend. We did not come to take anything from anyone. We came to teach them more. Imagine your mother's hair when it is in a braid; it takes three strands to make a braid, right? Well, people living in this Garden right now are viewing only two of the three, and you cannot make a braid with only two, right?'

"The three strands in the braid of which Yeshua spoke represent the Divine Mother, the Divine Father, and the Holy Spirit. In Yeshua's analogy, the missing strand was that of the Holy Spirit.

"Yeshua went on to say, 'Remember, we are not here to take away people's beliefs, we are here only to add to them, and people are free to choose what they feel supports them.'

"I believe Yeshua was showing us there was never a need to judge anyone for doing the 'wrong' thing. We came to infuse the Holy Spirit, symbolized by the dove: hence the Sisterhood of the Dove. With Miriyam as Yeshua's equal, she carried on with her part of the soul contract and birthed the energy of the Dove consciousness within this Garden.

"From the time shortly after Sarah was born until she was 30, Miriyam studied the ways of the Goddess in the library of Alexandria, in Egypt. Mary would send her there, while she tended to us.

"Mother would teleport for many of those times. When she was pregnant, she was not allowed to teleport, and the Hathors would take her in their flying ships. She left for what seemed like moments in this reality and studied for half suns in another reality.

"As much as I am telling you of her past, you must also know that Miriyam, as I said before, preferred the language of silence. There are many things she did not verbally pass on, including all that she went through on her different travels to gather the teachings of the Goddess.

"Another way she received her teaching was at night while she slept. The Hathors, the Sirians, and other beings of a similar nature would come in her dreamtime and remind her of the things she was to manifest. Miriyam would awaken with a lot of information at times; I was surprised that she did not have constant head pains."

Rachel breathed for a moment with her eyes closed, then said, "I was going to continue with the story but am being directed in this moment to stop for the night. Perhaps the Hathors will come and visit you tonight while you sleep. The Servers will lead you out through the Gateway of the Southeast with its symbols of the sun, the moon, and the stars atop it. The first evening you embraced the key of life, the second evening your inner male and female selves began to merge, and tonight you become aware of your part in the grand soul contract.

"Rise when you rise. Allow your body to monitor its own time. Servers, wake no one as they may be off gathering teachings from other dimensions. Arrive to your classes in your own flow, disrupt as little as possible, and trust in Nut's magnificent sky you see above us.

"Keep warm, children; the weather will not improve for a few suns. RA BA RA."

CHAPTER 4
MIRIYAM'S VISION BEGINS

R achel stood beside the sacred ceremonial pool located in the center of the temple; her eyes followed the pillar in its center up to the large, flawlessly polished, black stone, which lay upon an altar atop the pillar. One of the purposes of the stone was to capture the light from Sirius as it shone. The water in the pool absorbed the newly stored energy in the stone. Each would drink of the Goddess and her unconditional love during the initiation. The entire pool and the altar area had seven thin, tightly woven fabrics in the colors of the rainbow, brought from the Far East, and placed over it to maintain the cleanliness of the liquid.

The sacred liquid had several uses of which two

were: ceremonial purification and water for drinking. The water in the pool, refreshed by the sisters each new and full moon, was fed into the temple from the river, which lay a short distance outside the Gateway of the West.

As Rachel drank, she looked at each of the eight enormous arches, four of which were called gateways. Each arch had a unique symbol carved into its center, which reflected the qualities taught within the Sisterhood. Starting with the Eastern Gateway and moving clockwise around the temple, the first arch held the symbols of the dove and the rose. The dove was for the Holy Spirit, which represented absolute healing of the physical, emotional, and mental natures of human beings. The rose was a symbol of openness and surrender. Sisters were asked to model their behavior after the rose, opening themselves to the Holy Spirit as the rose opened itself to the sun. The second arch held the sun, the moon, and the stars. The sun symbolized the active, masculine principle within the universe, the moon symbolized the receptive, feminine principle within the universe, and the stars were present to remind the sisters that they were each an integral part of the grand tapestry of the Goddess. The third arch, the Gateway of the South, held the symbols of wheat and fruit. These were for prosperity, bounty, and nourishment, and were reminders to all that the Garden was their true provider. The fourth arch held the symbol of the olive branch, which stood for everlasting peace. The fifth arch, the Gateway of the West, held the sign of the six-pointed star. This symbol was formed by two interlocking, equilateral triangles facing in opposite directions. The triangle with its point facing downward symbolized the higher self entering human form. The triangle with its point facing upward symbolized the lower self ascending. As the lower rises and the upper descends, they form what is called a six-pointed star with the true heart of a human being at the center of the star. The sixth arch held the symbol of the chalice, the vessel that receives the spirit. When the human being, man or woman, embraces his or her inner Goddess he or she, in essence, becomes a chalice full of the eternal spirit. The seventh arch, the Gateway of the North, held the symbol of the ankh. The ankh is the symbol of the Goddess Isis and the key to eternal life. Lastly, the eighth arch held the sign of the Vesica Pisces. The Vesica Pisces, with its two perfectly interlocking rings, stood for perfect love and sacred union within the human form.

A dove landed upon Rachel's shoulder, interrupting her thoughts of appreciation for the labor of love her mother, grandmother, and countless others had put into the creation of the temple.

Soon the now silent temple would yield to the sounds of joy, laughter, storytelling, and celebration. Rachel walked to her seat and awaited her sisters. She sat bundled up, as it was a chilly evening.

SISTERHOOD OF THE DOVE

* * * * *

Gathered before her, the sisters sat huddled together. Rachel sent out a silent prayer to the Goddess asking that all would hear her this night and that she would be given a healing for her vocal cords. Rachel foresaw that tonight, tomorrow, and the night after that, would take a lot out of her. The weather always reflected the state of consciousness of the collective, and judging by the weather, this group before her was feeling emotional and mental unrest.

"Would the 12 sisters offering service during these ceremonies please stand." Twelve women rose and identified themselves. Each wore a blue scarf, embroidered with the white symbol of the dove. "Please acknowledge them for their wonderful service thus far and may I remind you that during our time together you will look upon these women as the Goddess Isis, who is ever available in service to your soul and spirit.

"Take the hand of your fellow sister." Rachel paused as they united. "Remember this moment, my children, for it is precious."

"During the past three nights, I have spoken much about Miriyam. She has assembled 10 of her 12 DNA strands. She has birthed five children, three with Yeshua. She has embraced her lessons of abuse, forgiveness, parenting, restriction, tolerance, fear, and more. Mary has taught her the ways of the Goddess as she herself was taught in the Temple of

Isis. Yeshua has guided her upon the path of unconditional love as brought forth from the Magi and his inner connection with the Divine.

"Tonight, however, I shall speak of other things relevant to our story, things of this world and things not of this world."

Rachel gently leaned forward, drawing the listeners in. "Where does one begin a story in which there is no beginning? I suppose one begins somewhere in the middle and that is exactly what I did three nights ago. This part of the story begins long before any of us were born. One might say that this story begins in the Heaven world, and in this Heaven world a group of beings is choosing a course of action that has not been attempted since Queen Nefertiti, King Akhenaten, and their son, the future king, Tutankhamun[29], walked in the Land of Egypt.

"The group of which I am speaking I shall call The Council. The Council has within it members of almost every race within our universe, and when I say almost every race, I mean many beings from what we would refer to as the stars. Many of you are aware that we, as human beings, are not the only race. We are but one race within an entire Galactic Federation that spans the seen and the unseen. A few races have refused to join The Council. Of significance to our story is a race known as the Anunnaki.

"The Anunnaki have, for a long time, held an influence over our Garden, an influence that many people experience as fear, jealousy, power, and control. With the poisoning of young King Tutankhamun, the Anunnaki's influence grew significantly over the peoples and their Garden. This influence went unchallenged for 1,400 festivals. During that time span, The Council honored, respected, and allowed human beings to create their free will – to awaken spiritually under the influence of the Anunnaki – because of the Garden's collective choice to remove the young King from life. As I mentioned, these are the influencing energies of fear, jealousy, power, and control, all of which were a part of King Tutankhamun's death. With great love, The Council did not interfere with the lessons of this Garden and an arrangement was made with the Anunnaki.

"Periodically within that time period, during Council gatherings, members would speak of the Garden and the choice her peoples had made. During those times, The Council would choose whether or not to become involved in Her happenings.

"I have given you a tiny bit regarding events that happened and continue to happen. This is relevant to the next part of the story I will tell. It is relevant to why the soul group of 22 incarnated, for The Council decided it was time for a cleansing."

Rachel shifted in her chair, signifying a shift in direction. "How many of you met with the Hathors last night?" Cautiously, about 300 hands went up. "Good, that makes my task simpler. And how many glimpsed their soul contract?" About 200 hands went up, including the hand of almost every child.

"For those of you who have not glimpsed your soul contract, give your fears to the Goddess Isis and allow her to carry them off with the winds of change."

Rachel gathered her energy inward for a moment.

"Now I shall share an overview of some of the happenings in Judah during the 18 moons that my father, Yeshua, was away from us.

"On and off, Miriyam and the community would hear news of Yeshua's cousin John. People were calling him The Baptist. A rumor was going around that John was awaiting the Messiah and that he was baptizing people in preparation. I met John when I was four and he baptized me and everyone else in the caravan traveling with us.

"Mother described John to me saying, 'He is his own being, a nomad, and he preaches and travels around the countryside. He is similar to your father.'

"John was more of a loner than Yeshua was, however. He loved spreading the word of God. John always remembered his part of the soul contract; he was one of the soul group of 22, and he was waiting for the prophecy of God to be fulfilled: the part in the sacred scrolls which refers to the time when the Messiah will come.

"The Anunnaki-Sanhedrin were busy hunting the Essene people down, and, for this reason, John was sending forth the message in symbolic ways. He knew that the Messiah he was awaiting was not one man. He recalled that the Messiah aspect of the soul contract was about the soul group of 22, but the mass consciousness of people did not know this; they were waiting for one man, so John spoke to them in the language they understood."

At that moment, in the middle of the crowd, Rachel saw a hand go up. The woman spoke, "I am not following how the Anunnaki influence us. You said the Anunnaki-Sanhedrin; how does one tell the difference between someone who is influenced by the Anunnaki and someone who is not?"

Rachel sighed, looking out at the nodding heads of the *sisters*. "Are there others here who desire to go into this now?" Rachel asked, desiring not to spend the time on this subject herself. She, however, was in service, and therefore allowed the collective to choose.

Approximately 300 raised their hands. Rachel nodded and contemplated where to start. "This discussion is much more appropriately done in the classes with your teachers, but I shall lightly cover this subject with you.

"As I mentioned, the Anunnaki are a non-human race of beings that use the energies of fear, jealousy, power, and control to influence humankind. The human being who masters these lessons remains unaffected. The human being currently growing and learning the lessons of fear, jealousy, power, and control is already under the influence of the

Anunnaki, but may, in any moment, liberate himself or herself because, as human beings, we have the gift of free will and we may use our free will to choose love, compassion, mercy, and tolerance. Every moment is a choice, children. The Anunnaki know that every moment is a choice and work tirelessly to see that you forget this. In addition, with this poor memory instilled, they hint for you to give your power of choice away.

"The Anunnaki, being non-human, do not have physical bodies as we do. They choose not to incarnate as we have but to over-shadow and possess those who have incarnated. They specifically choose human beings who have any or all of these qualities active in their lives; if they are in a place of leadership then it is all the better, for they often choose imbalanced leaders of countries and religions, people in places of authority.

"This Garden is a place of duality. The Anunnaki are of one polarity. The other group, The Builders, whom I have not named until now, is of the other. The Anunnaki support separation, domination, giving one's power away to an outside source, and becoming a slave to the five senses. The Builders support unity, unconditional love, freedom, and a life of liberation from the five senses.

"I trust this to be helpful and not more confusing. Breathe in this teaching now as I continue the story."

Rachel waited for them to take in what she had shared before continuing. "While Yeshua was away over that 18-moon period, I continued to become aware, in my own little way, of his popularity. Miriyam told me, in the times to follow, that he was raising the consciousness of people and of humanity so rapidly, that they were starting to see for themselves, 'We can do this. We do not have to be bound by religion and the Sanhedrin; we need not be bound by this type of tradition. We are much bigger. We may choose to be free spirits and recognize that we are divine.'

"While Yeshua was traveling, studying, teaching, and living his part of the soul contract, the other 21 continued gathering the teachings they needed to bring the soul contract to fruition.

"King Herod was increasing taxes and the changes being made in the country irked the Essene community. The more the changes took place the more we became secluded and the less we ventured up to Jerusalem; the less the entire community went out. The Anunnaki, working through the Sanhedrin and King Herod, did not force us into seclusion; we chose it.

"A group of people wanted to overthrow the government. Because of this, the Anunnaki-Sanhedrin kept a watchful eye upon the Essene community. They felt the Essene people were riling up the country in an effort to overthrow the government.

"As many of you know, the peoples of Judah are separated into four sects. These sects are the Pharisees, the Sadducees, the Essene, and the

Zealots. It may be noteworthy for some of you to study this political structure to pass along to the younger generations. If this feels like something worth doing, then you may study it with the teachers in the suns to come. I have reserved this phase of the moon, however, for teachings of another sort.

"One of the key ways the Anunnaki manipulate energy is to make people live in areas where they will be in constant fear. For example, in areas where there are mudslides, people may allow themselves to be controlled by their government; they may be dependant upon their government. The Roman people placed Herod in the position of king so that the Jews would still think that they had a country. The Roman people collectively governed everything, while the Sanhedrin and the King dealt with Jewish law. The raise in taxes was, in part, because King Herod needed his tax and the Roman people needed theirs.

"It is important to remember the magnitude of what the soul group of 22 are involved in. These 22 are master beings, come to mirror to the world its plight, and offer to the people the opportunity of liberation from the influence of the Anunnaki. The Sanhedrin is full of Anunnaki. They took over the bodies of King Herod and his wife. Some here have met Salomé, the queen's daughter; she was under the influence of the Anunnaki at that time as well.

"Yeshua was not all right with this; in fact, the entire Essene community was not all right with it.

SISTERHOOD OF THE DOVE

We were much more into bartering than we were into purchasing things. The Anunnaki-Roman people were the ones creating the money and the coins, and getting people more involved with buying and selling, and using money as the commodity.

"We, the Essenes, were about exchanging energy; *who you are becomes important*, not *if you have or do not have*.

"It would be much later that Yeshua would turn the Holy Temple upside down for selling merchandise and creating profits through the consciousness of greed in the sacred temples.

"One of the key teachings of the Essene is sacredness. One must work from one's connection with the divine, one's partnership with the divine, and in that partnership with the divine all one's needs will be met.

"The Anunnaki sought to use people in order to take advantage of the sacred to make money. In order to control people, they disconnected them from the divine through the introduction of materialism.

"Yeshua told a parable of these times later during his travels. It was late afternoon and the people had gathered to listen to him speak. He hinted about many things to come and gave this teaching while he shared. *'It is easier for a camel to go through the eye of a needle, than for a rich man to enter into the kingdom of God.'*

"When he said this you need to understand that

in the Kabbalistic knowing, *Gimal*, the third letter of the alphabet, means *camel* and represents the reality of the third dimension. The Kabbalists would speak this way for people to understand certain conditions. What I believe he was saying is that it is easier to go through the third dimension to the gateway, symbolized by the eye of the needle, and onto and through different dimensional portal-ways, than it is to separate a rich man from his belongings.

"One must transcend the third dimension, and release one's attachment to the five senses, in order to move through the gateway. He was saying that this is easier to do, than to separate a rich man from his belongings."

Rachel paused at this point, listening to her inner guidance. "My throat needs rest," she shared, recalling that to nurture herself sets an example for her sisters. "Thus my story concludes early tonight. Keep warm, children. Tonight you are to choose a new location and a new direction in which to rest your head. Mothers, your children are not to sleep with you tonight unless you are nursing. Servers, see them out the Gateway of the South with its symbols of fruit and wheat. May you detach from the fruit of your womb, may you embrace the ever-present, bountiful spirit of the Goddess, and may your soul be nourished and readied for service. We shall reunite parent and child when Ra has awoken. Much love, children. RA BA RA"

Rachel watched as they left and made her way to the sacred pool of water in the center of the temple. She offered prayers to Isis, and, as she turned to leave, she was overjoyed to be standing face to face with a Crone. She had listened to her mother tell of the Crones: beings in female form who were Guardians of the Garden throughout time. The Crone appeared at the temple during each Festival. For all Rachel knew, this being was born at the same time as the Garden was born. The Crone had been coming to the temple site long before a temple had ever been erected and Rachel always felt truly blessed to see her.

"She has your father's eyes," Rachel recalled her mother saying, "very familiar." Miriyam also said of her, "She must be Isis in her Crone form."

The Crone lifted one of the veils covering the pool, placed her hands in the water, and anointed Rachel upon her forehead with the symbol of the sacred spiral. Rachel's body, mind, and heart expanded immediately and she felt herself as a dove in flight.

Moments later a tender embrace had Rachel back in her body. The Crone wished her well, and walked off in the direction of the east. The Gateway of the East was the temple entrance and therefore it was not customary for one to leave in this manner, as it is where the Light of the Sun God Ra's first rays flow into the temple. The sisters would leave the temple through the Gateway of the West, unless otherwise instructed. When one left by way of the Gateway of the East, it sent forth a message that one was not really leaving.

Rachel made her way from the temple and, as she neared the rest area, one of the Servers brought her a hot cup of tea made of licorice, marshmallow, slippery elm, and mullein. Rachel thanked her, and, as the Server left, she sipped her tea, recalling her husband, Daniel, and the number of times he would bring her tea in their little, stone dwelling. They had lived in it for 30 festivals now. It was built in the classic Priestess style: rounded, with no corners, as corners created a stagnancy of energy. Theirs was a community that respected the natural flow of the universe and there is nothing worse to the soul than the experience of stagnation.

As the tea gently coated her throat, she recalled saying goodbye to him. "I shall return on the 11th sun," she had said as she threw on her shawl, picked up the items she had prepared the night before, and, grabbing her walking stick, kissed him goodbye.

She recalled how beautiful the walk to the temple was that morning. She was the first to arrive and she spent two nights in the temple by herself. Throughout those suns, she treasured her time preparing the temple grounds in silence as she had watched her mother do festival after festival. During mid-morning of the third sun, her *sisters* arrived.

An owl's song gently brought her to the present. Rachel rinsed her cup in the river and made for her bed-mat.

CHAPTER 5
"WHEN ONE SUFFERS..."

The weather had not improved; in fact, it had become worse. To add to the cold, which had been present for the last two nights, a storm was threatening. Lightening flashed in the distance and thunder sang her song of balance and equilibrium. The winds had picked up and Rachel wondered if her voice would continue to hold out. She wasted little time, desiring to get this part of story in before the weather became worse. As she readied herself to speak, Rachel heard the voice of Isis. "I will keep the rains at a distance this night. I shall clear the air with light and sound only. Prepare for a water cleansing tomorrow."

Rachel paused a moment until she had the

listeners attention.

"It was during the evening of Yeshua's return, after the healing of Binyamin, and after the two of them had put us to sleep that they went outside and sat together under the stars. The weather was becoming colder and Miriyam draped her shawl around herself. She said to him, 'I have had visions of you and me, visions of our country and visions of the state of our people: what do they mean? Is what I have seen going to happen?'

"Yeshua looked at her in that tender way he had and spoke these words with the deepest love and the strongest of commitments, 'Remember the soul contract, Miriyam; it is bigger than the two of us. Do not falter into the role of the wife; remember, we are equal. Remember also that when I suffer, you will find joy. Remember the soul contract.'

"She stood weeping as he held her; then they joined in loving tantra under the stars and Miriyam merged her 11th strand of DNA.

"Shortly after this night, Yeshua informed us that he would leave again, this time for six moons. He told us that he was headed into the Sinai by himself. This was unusual; he had never gone off by himself before. He informed Miriyam that the 12th Magus was calling him and that he must travel this journey by himself. He also mentioned that while away, he would be out of touch. There would be no meeting in the inner worlds during this time.

"Yeshua had his greatest challenge during those six moons. I would have thought it to be at another point in his life, but apparently, after he had met with the 12th Magus and spoken to several groups of people, the Magus sent him out into the desert to face the final remnants of fear within his body. Upon another level Yeshua was highly evolved, but when he came into this density of body, which has great fear in the mass consciousness, it created a shadow, which he chose to embrace. The Anunnaki sent forth the materialization of one of their greatest warriors to be with Yeshua for a period of 40 suns as he integrated his 12th stand of DNA.

"When Yeshua returned, he was glowing as I had never seen before. Before his return, Miriyam had prepared the entire caravan because the Goddess told her, 'Prepare those who feel called to travel upon Yeshua's return.'

"Yeshua told us that we would be traveling inside the country and that we would be going to Jerusalem on this trip. I was happy about that because we had not traveled to Jerusalem in a long time. Little did I know that it would take as long as it did to get there.

"Rivka and Baruch chose not to travel with us; they stayed with the Essene community.

"Within a few suns the caravan was ready for departure, and about 35 of us left the Essene community. From time to time, Uncle Joseph joined us, but mostly he kept to his business and travels. Whenever he did appear, Sarah was always the first in line to embrace him. Their soul bond manifests as one of the strongest I have ever seen.

"Of auspicious note upon our journey was the time we entered Canaan. We were invited to a wedding and Mary came to Yeshua saying that the family of the wedding party had run out of wine; she wanted him to manifest some to ease the burden of the father of the bride, and to create the sacredness of the wedding.

"Yeshua responded by saying, 'You know I am not to come out in the open yet.'

"But if anyone here has ever met Mary, then you will know how persistent she is and not even Yeshua would say no to her in that moment. In the soul contract, however, it was the Goddess moving through Mary, urging Yeshua that it was time for him to present to the world the limitless manifestation of God.

"That night Yeshua created what people called a miracle, and the word went out, traveling far and wide, of the man who turned water into wine.

"We continued with our travel, and as we continued, our caravan grew. People joined us at each stop; they wanted to be around Yeshua. It was around this time that we began to meet additional members of the soul group of 22.

"Our caravan arrived at the Jordan River with about 100 people. Yeshua pointed out his cousin John to us; this visit was the first and last time I saw John. He did not see Yeshua right away and I had the feeling that this was how Yeshua wanted it.

"Yeshua explained that we would all be dipped into the water and receive baptism. He said that the

Spirit of the Dove would enter us and that each of our lives would change. He reminded us of the analogy he had shared of the Holy Spirit.

"Yeshua rose and we all followed as he led us down to the river. When John looked into the eyes of Yeshua, Yeshua transmitted the energy of the Magi, and, for a moment, John froze. I imagine that he saw the full plan for his life and was inspired by the love of Yeshua to carry it through. He came over and the two embraced. I heard John say, 'My job is done.'

"Yeshua asked him if he would baptize us and John seemed surprised by his request. But that afternoon John baptized the entire caravan.

"That evening, we met the first of the ones who would later be known as the Apostles. They were over by the Kinneret[30], fishing with their nets.

"By this time, Yeshua was about 30 when he began to draw these men to him, and the last of the 12 *brothers*, as he called them, was gathered within 12 moons. Just as Yeshua had met the Magi over a specific period, the members representing his *brothers* from the soul group were drawn to him in a similar way.

"The soul contract was written so that 12 of the 22 souls would mirror to the peoples of this Garden the 12 lessons that stood in each person's way of reconnecting their own 12 strands of DNA.

"Each of the 12 made this choice before incarnation, to take on a specific challenge, which represented, to each human being, what stood between them and realizing themselves as manifested God beings who remembered their origins. The 12 lessons Yeshua's *brothers* mirrored to the peoples of this Garden were: Initiative, Dependability, Flexibility, Nurturance, Courage, Organization, Balance, Transformation, Philosophy, Responsibility, Community, and Vision.

"If this teaching is to have any value, then one must understand that in the world in which we live, nothing is written in stone, because we have free will, and although Yeshua and Miriyam saw a probable outcome for humanity, they firmly held to the belief that, in the blink of an eye, awareness might come.

"Knowing this, one may understand when I say that there was more than one outcome written into the soul contract. The death and ascension of Yeshua were not the only outcomes.

"We as humans--and I say *we* because we are all here in this Garden at this time, and must take responsibility, whether we are acting for the Light of the Goddess or for the Shadow of the Anunnaki-- we must all take responsibility for this Garden's seeming successes or failures. As part of the collective whole, each incarnated soul is responsible for the outcome. Never say, 'I chose this or I did not choose that.' We all chose it because we are all part of the collective consciousness within this Garden and to think differently supports the view of separation, which supports the Anunnaki. Yeshua once said, 'Praise and blame are but the same.'

"If we, the peoples of this Garden, having not given our power to the Anunnaki-Sanhedrin, had chosen more of the spirituality and less of the dogma, then there still would have been a chance to fully anchor the soul contract for which the soul group of 22 came forth, without the lesson of the crucifixion, the lesson of deception, and the lesson of betrayal.

"Yeshua taught unity and through his instruction I know that I crucified my own father, that we all crucified him. He taught, 'I am that.' He taught that when one looks upon this Garden, one sees separation all around. One may think, 'I am me and you are you,' but this is not so. What is so is, 'I am that.' When one looks upon one's neighbor, the neighbor may seem good or bad, honest or dishonest, but in truth, 'I am that good, I am that bad, I am that honesty, and I am that dishonesty.'

"In truth, I am my father who was crucified that day, and I am the Anunnaki who saw to the crucifixion; 'I am that.' There is nothing that I am not, nothing that we all are not."

Rachel looked out at her sisters, watching their energy as they received her words. "Hear me, children; there is nothing that we are not. I request that you look around yourselves now: look out at the things you think are separate from you; look out at the things you judge as good and bad and say to yourself, 'I am that. I am that. I am that I AM.'

"News came to us that John the Baptist had died within a few moons after baptizing us. Yeshua and

Miriyam knew it was going to happen. A possibility existed, however, of altering his death if we, the people, had made another choice. John knew that the Anunnaki were overshadowing King Herod and his wife; he knew that their tool was to create fear in the peoples so that they would agree to be controlled. John agreed to show the people how vulnerable they were. It was another attempt by the soul group to offer grace to the people by showing them how the Anunnaki worked and how, by following the Divine, they might free themselves.

"John was beheaded by the king at the request of his wife. Part of the symbolism of John's teachings was to show that fear takes place in the mind. That is one of the reasons he baptized people, saying, place your head below your feelings; place your mind below your heart. With his agreement to have his head severed, or, as many believe, by sacrificing his own head, he was releasing that part of the being which creates judgment, which is busy in the outside world. Understand that fear creates judgment, children.

"King Herod's wife, being of the Anunnaki, was mirroring the consciousness of the people who did not want to look into themselves; she did not want to look into herself. Instead, she sought out and got John's head, using her own daughter, Salome, to achieve this.

"Salome realized that John was a holy man and that she had allowed her mother to manipulate her into asking for his head. As she continued to gaze at

John, his head on the block," Rachel took a breath and continued speaking, "She felt a shift in her spirit, an awakening, as if a cloud had been released.

"When we went back to Jerusalem, Salome sought us out and asked for permission to travel with us. She no longer fit with the royal family, as she had freed herself from the influence of the Anunnaki. Miriyam, without hesitation, welcomed her as one of her own, and later Salome became part of the Sisterhood.

"Miriyam said of Yeshua's 12 *brothers*, 'Because their part of the soul contract demanded that they mirror the particular challenge of each DNA strand to humankind, they must accept this dense part of humanity into themselves. Knowing this helped me to love each one without judgment, for, in truth, they were only mirroring back to humankind its choices and fulfilling their missions. Many of Yeshua's *brothers* were conditioned by Judaism, and, because of this, they believed in keeping the males separate from the females. For this reason it was difficult for them to look at me as Yeshua's equal. They were not Essene, and they were bothered by Yeshua's treatment of me as his equal. They felt that Yeshua would lose the respect of the people if he held me close to him. I attended many of the meetings and he turned to me often for insight. Mary attended some of those meetings as well. Particular meetings the public attended, and at times women were present. In the beginning, many of his *brothers* were not in favor of this. Yeshua, however, paid no mind to this aspect of their behavior. I, too, paid no mind to it and instead chose to look at them with compassion, as they were becoming aware of the light within themselves, as I had only a short while ago.'

"You may desire to know that three of Yeshua's 12 *brothers* were married and only one of the wives joined her husband; she had no children.

"Binyamin was five at this time and attended most of the meetings with Yeshua. Binyamin was bright, and loved being around him. He would drink in everything that Yeshua said. Miriyam described him as behaving like a puppy, the way he would follow Yeshua around. Binyamin loved male companionship; He did not mind females, but he preferred to be around the men. While Binyamin was with the men, I spent much of my time learning from Mary the ways of the Goddess. As for Sarah, she continuously found her teachings in nature.

"Before our baptism by John, Yeshua and Miriyam stopped teleporting. She was in her mid-20s and he was about 30. Following the baptism, Yeshua and Miriam chose to live from the heart up. They had merged their 12 strands of DNA and chose to no longer join together in a tantric way."

Rachel took in the weather around her. "With the mass consciousness of people staying relatively the same – forgetful in the *fog* created by the Anunnaki – Yeshua became aware that it was time to enter Jerusalem. Spring was upon us and we left Nazareth, arriving in Jerusalem a few suns before Pesach.

"Father knew that the season of spring equated to the direction of the east and was the gateway of spirit. The Dove of Peace desired to awaken the memory while the peoples of this Garden were facing in an easterly direction. On the outskirts of town, we all stopped for the night. We had enough light to continue and I was annoyed because I really wanted to get to Jerusalem. Yeshua sat and comforted me, telling me that I would do well to let go of my attachment to things within this Garden. I gave him a look that a child gives a parent when they want what they want regardless of the expense. He smiled and hugged me.

"Morning came and when I awoke I saw Yeshua all dressed up in white. It was odd. I knew I would not get an answer as to why he had dressed in white and chose to leave it alone.

"As we approached the edge of the city, Yeshua asked his brother James to bring him one of the white donkeys from the caravan. Uncle James did and Yeshua mounted it; he rode into Jerusalem upon its back. I knew of the writings in the sacred scrolls of the Messiah who would enter the Holy City riding upon a white donkey. I knew Yeshua was a special man but he was still my father and he treated us all like the Messiah. Later, Miriyam would tell me how upset the Anunnaki-Sanhedrin became after he did this.

"It was the Tuesday before Pesach and Yeshua took Miriyam up to the Garden of Gethsemane. He looked at her and said, 'Your visions are going to come true.' The two held each other and cried. He cried for humanity; she cried for humanity and for their relationship, thinking, 'We could have moved much easier to a better place if we, the people, had chosen to focus on love, on unity, and on community.' In that moment, she felt that for the time being, the Anunnaki had won because they, the people, were about to kill the heart, symbolized by Yeshua.

"Mother said they hoped that once they entered Jerusalem, and once the people looked into Yeshua's eyes as a collective, things would change. They did not and so they went to the Garden of Gethsemane, and sat and spoke and cried.

"Someone once asked Miriyam if they felt like failures and she replied calmly, 'No! There is a certain peace that comes with letting go.' It would be a long time before I understood how she might say this.

"On Wednesday night, Yeshua said his goodbyes to us, although, at the time, I had no idea that that is what he was doing. I realized it only shortly after he left his body. He said goodbye in this way, 'I will always be with you; you know that, you need only talk to me and you will feel me around you.' We thought it was another one of his teachings; little did we know the weight it would carry.

"Pesach began on Thursday. The entire community participated in the celebration. The building we went to had two levels and the immediate family, along with Yeshua's 12 *brothers*, were on the upper floor, while the rest of the people were on the main floor. Yeshua sat with Miriyam to his right, and Judas, one of his 12 *brothers,* to his left, in the middle of a long table. The rest of his *brothers* sat on either side of them. Four or five long tables at a 90-degree angle to the main table held the rest of the guests. We sat with Mary at one of those tables.

"I love the celebration of Pesach. Not only is it the time of my birth, but it is also the time we, as Jews, express gratitude for our freedom from slavery and the exodus from the Land of Egypt. Yeshua said the blessings and the children read from the sacred scrolls.

"When I was little, Miriyam would put us to bed with stories of her sacred union; part of the story involved a chalice from which she and Yeshua had drunk to receive the blessing. She told us that this chalice was special, but remained vague about its appearance. The only two things she constantly shared were about the stones upon it, and the weight of it. Therefore, when Yeshua lifted the chalice for the blessing and filled it for Elijah, those stories came back to me.

"Later I asked Miriyam, with my brother and sister present, if the chalice on the table that night in Jerusalem was similar to the one from which she had drunk upon her sacred union.

"'The only similarity between the two was that they represented the Goddess,' Miriyam said. She told us of two chalices: one fashioned from the elements of the Garden and one fashioned from a metal that did not exist within the Garden, one elaborate and one simple. She said that, if Yeshua had been crowned King, then the chalice from the time of their sacred union would have been brought to the Holy Temple in Jerusalem.

"When Sarah grew older, Uncle Joseph took her to the place along the Rose Line where she had been conceived. They meant to retrieve the chalice from under the oak tree but did not find it.

"With the Seder complete, Mary prepared us for sleep.

"Shortly after we left, Judas left the table and walked out. Miriyam looked at Yeshua, he nodded, and her heart plummeted because she knew that the time for him to leave drew near. Nausea filled her and she silently wept. Yeshua tenderly took her hand and held it under the table. As soon as he did so, everything in her body returned to center; she realized that he had placed her to his right so that she would receive his energy. The energy seemed to say, 'hold strong and become the joy while I suffer.'

"Yeshua had been adamant throughout their time together that she keep holding to the seed that they, the soul group of 22, were here to sow. Even if the Anunnaki were taking the active principle away, then the receptive principle was still present. In this way, the door would remain open, and the Anunnaki might win this round, but they would not win the game. In squeezing Miriyam's hand, Yeshua was giving her a good-bye hug; she held his hand as long and as tightly as she dared. He left shortly, and after that she saw him only in captivity.

"Yeshua left with his *brothers* to study the Torah for the night as his ancestors had done each Pesach. They were 12 that night, instead of 13, as Judas had not returned. Yeshua led them up to Mt. Olive and to the Garden of Gethsemane. Miriyam stayed with us, then put us to sleep and sat with Mary, and a few other women, who were talking excitedly about the fact that Yeshua had returned to Jerusalem. They seemed certain that Yeshua would become King.

"After that, Mary and Miriyam sat in silence, never saying in words, but each seeming to know, what was about to happen.

"Miriyam wanted to fight for her husband, wanted to grieve the way that a wife ought to grieve. Yet, having received his energy and remembering the soul contract, she felt no grief, only love.

"The Roman guards apprehended Yeshua early Friday morning. They took him not only because the Anunnaki-Sanhedrin needed to save face, but also because it was the sun before the Sabbath.

"Miriyam tried to find Yeshua, as she longed to be taken with him, to be held captive beside him; but the Roman guards denied her, pushing her away. She screamed out in agony to Yeshua, 'If I am your equal, then why am I not there with you?'

"In response she heard a voice as clear as crystal, 'In equality between two beings there is a balance: one must suffer the pain, while the other must carry on with joy.'

"This was to be one of Miriyam's greatest tests because she did not choose joy in that moment; she had already gone to the place of pain.

"Miriyam carried on because she knew her part of the soul contract. And, she knew that it was what Yeshua would want of her: to support all of the lessons and the whole mission of the soul group, without becoming caught up in the human mind. Instead, the soul group was to hold to a higher mind, and it was this that Miriyam taught Sarah, Binyamin and me. By becoming the equal of Yeshua, whatever he held, she held. There was no loss for my siblings and me because where ever he was, she was. The energy of the divine was intermingled between them. She told us, 'As he bled, I bled. As he died, I died. As I lived, he lived. When he ascended, I, too, ascended.'

"During the nights, Yeshua would come to Miriyam on the inner and they would talk. Sarah and Binyamin had had dreams of him. I was hurt because he did not come to me in the dreamtime.

"It was Saturday morning when Joseph arrived at the temple. He had been out of town and come back as quickly as possible. He spoke to the Roman people in charge, and began the fight to save

Yeshua from the false charges brought against him.

"As I said, it was on the eve of the Sabbath that Father was returned to the Jews and it was on this night that Pontius Pilate asked the people, 'Who do you want freed? Do you want us to free your king, Yeshua, or do you want us to free this thief, Barabbas?' The people chose Barabbas.

"Yeshua was taken by the Anunnaki who possessed King Herod and the Sanhedrin. During the trial of Yeshua, Joseph used his influence and wealth to mount a defense that had the Anunnaki-Sanhedrin backing up on their heels. They demanded that Yeshua deny that he was the Messiah. He would not and did not.

"None of his 12 *brothers* came to his trial, because they were afraid. Their human density had come forth and the challenging part of their DNA took over the moment Yeshua was apprehended. Each began mirroring to the peoples of this Garden what was taking place within themselves[31].

"All disappeared except Uncle James, who comforted Mary. We spent our time praying and heard what happened only from other people. Miriyam heard from Yeshua in the dreamtime. He never said much about what was going on where he was, but continually shared his love.

"It was only after the people had made their choice to free the thief that Yeshua said to Joseph, 'The people have made their choice. They would have a thief as King. They would enslave the Kingdom of God.'

"Yeshua saw that the people would not stand up for the Kingdom of God and told Joseph to fight and fight well. Joseph saw in Yeshua's eyes that they would lose. He put up a valiant effort for the few in the crowd who did want the Kingdom of God. Yeshua's mission was clear now and he surrendered to teaching the people in other ways. He asked Joseph to care for us, his family: 'Tend to Sarah, and take her where she must go. Tend to Miriyam, for she will continue the teachings. Tend to Rachel, and tell her that she is greatly loved. Tend to Binyamin and teach him the ways of the world, for he was brought forth to unite the old school with the new. And tell my mother that I love her.'

"On Sunday morning, Yeshua carried the cross through the streets. Mary, James, and Miriyam prayed with and for him as he walked. My siblings and I were not allowed to go. Miriyam did not want us to see what would happen to Yeshua; they had agreed in the dreamtime that this was the best thing for us. Sarah did not listen, however; she left her body and watched everything from that dimension. Binyamin and I prayed and cried, as we knew our father would not return.

"He stopped 13 times before he reached Mt. Golgotha. Miriyam said it was as though different parts of him were coming together to deal with what was about to take place. She said she saw two of him at times; She saw him when he was leaving his body and she saw him when he was coming back to it. She felt he was saying to the people that they had betrayed the Goddess, that each stop he made represented one of the 13 moons, and that, with each stop, he gave them a moment to reflect upon their choice; when they did not get it, he moved on.

"Yeshua arrived at Mt. Golgotha, collapsing as the wood crashed to the ground. Miriyam watched as he allowed himself to be laid atop the cross. He did not look at her. While standing there, watching her husband as his wrists and feet were pierced with thick spikes, she felt tremendous support, as if all of the angels she had ever known were keeping her on her feet. She wanted to collapse, but the Goddess held her spine perfectly erect and, with each nail hammered into her beloved, he did not utter a word. She became aware that the Romans had lost the fifth and final nail to drive into his chest and she recalled the sacred scrolls, which said that the heart of a saint would never be touched.

"As she stood there, she became a witness, totally devoid of emotion. With each nail, she felt internal physical pain and yet her spirit remained untouched. Mary, James, and she stood perfectly erect, holding the energy of the Goddess to support Yeshua in his transition.

"Two other men were crucified alongside Yeshua that day. Each had nails hammered through their chests. Miriyam watched as one of them spoke to Yeshua. She saw that this man instantly felt calmed by his response.

"Yeshua did not look at her until the Romans

had erected the cross, and even then looked her way only once. As he did so, she felt immense love flowing between them. He said many things while on the cross that first hour. He recited 10 Psalms[32]. He recited the Tikunim[33].

"Shortly after he finished his prayers, Mary, James, and she heard, at the same moment, 'move to the other side.' Miriyam resisted; she did not want to leave him. She was being told to move around behind him; She eventually surrendered and moved to the back of the cross. As soon as she did, the sky darkened and opened; rain poured forth, thunder echoed, and, in that moment, a lightening bolt exploded at the base of the rock where Miriyam and the others had stood. The land shook and quaked with the explosion.

"As John the Baptist had sacrificed his own, the entire nation had sacrificed its head, its King. The peoples of this Garden had allowed the Anunnaki the upper hand. But the Garden would not participate in this public display of injustice. She shared the rage of her fire, the tears of her grief, and the voice of her being. At that moment the sky turned dark, chaos ensued, and people started running away."

Rachel looked at the sisters, then up to the sky. She saw the clouds hiding the stars of Nut.

"Isis is using the weather to heal us, children. Exit through the Gateway of the Southwest, with its symbol of the olive branch representing eternal peace; breathe this peace in as the Servers hand you each an olive branch. Swiftly now, children, swiftly: it may rain at any moment. RA BA RA."

A woman came to Rachel on her way out and offered compassion for the loss of Yeshua.

"I do miss holding him," Rachel answered, "but he is not gone and I have no sense of emotional loss. He is ever present."

CHAPTER 6
"...ONE MUST CARRY ON WITH JOY."

They were all about to get wet. In meditation, Isis transmitted to Rachel that the temple grounds were in need of a cleansing and tonight would be the night. Those present were well into the process of releasing the Anunnaki influence of fear, jealousy, power, and control. These dense vibrations hung in the air throughout the temple and its grounds. It was up to the sisters to allow themselves to be rained on. If they joined in the energy of joy, then the rains would hold off until the end of the storytelling this night and Rachel's vocal cords would heal. If they stayed in the energy of suffering, then Rachel's vocal cords would become unusable and the rains would cleanse them during the storytelling, drawing their evening together to an early close.

As she entered the temple, Rachel saw the sisters wrapped in their blankets, dedicated to their path of service, and eager to hear how Miriyam carried on with joy.

Rachel sat and began, "After Yeshua left the Seder table the night of Pesach, Thursday, and went out with his *brothers* to the Garden of Gethsemane to pray, Miriyam's menses began to flow. She felt that it was her body's way of crying, mourning, and releasing in the way of the Goddess.

"She stopped bleeding the moment Yeshua left his body.

"Also, Joseph gave Miriyam and Mary the messages Yeshua had asked him to deliver during the trial.

"When Yeshua drew his last breath, Miriyam was filled with anger and pain and said, 'It was as if I was allowed, at that moment, to feel it all, and then it was gone.'

"Miriyam and the others had returned to the front of the cross. Few people stayed upon the hill, and when Yeshua had left his body, Joseph asked a soldier to take it down.

"Miriyam's heart was happy that Yeshua did not stay long in suffering. She knew that he had willed himself to leave. The men to his left and right had died also.

"The soldier agreed to bring him down but said

that he must first confirm that Yeshua was indeed dead. At that point, he walked up the hill and pierced the side of Yeshua's body with his spear. The cross was lowered and they moved his body to one of the tombs that Joseph owned.

"Miriyam and Mary applied the sacred oils to Yeshua's body and left Joseph in the tomb to return to my siblings and me. After Miriyam had tried her best to console us, she returned to the cave, as it is tradition to be with the dead for an entire sun. Once she had left, she did not return until she was complete. She stayed inside of the cave with Yeshua for all of that time while Joseph stayed outside, keeping watch. Upon the following sun, he brought water and bread into the cave for her to eat, but she did not want any.

"'Please Miriyam, you need your strength,' he begged. She eventually surrendered and ate a small portion. Shortly after she finished, Joseph said, 'It's time to leave." They walked out of the cave and the men rolled a large rock over its entrance.

"Miriyam and Joseph returned home. She made sure we were well and then left by herself to return to the cave. The next sun, Wednesday, she returned again, and as she approached the cave, she saw that the rock had been moved to the side. She went into the cave, and when she saw that Yeshua's body was not there she thought, 'The Romans have taken my husband's body.' She realized a moment later, however, that there were no guards anywhere outside the cave.

"Miriyam began to run back to get Joseph and while she was running, she said, 'That's when I saw him. He manifested in front me, and he was as real as I am looking at you. I was so happy to see him back. I ran with enthusiasm to hold him again. My heart was overflowing and the emotional void that had been within me lifted. He raised his hand, outstretched, for me to stop. An energy field came from his hand as he spoke, 'Come back to your center, woman.' He did not allow me to touch him at first. We spoke as we walked next to each other heading back to the house.

"'We arrived back to the *family* and all but Mary were asleep. They had been sitting Shivaah, all in the same room, and, as we walked in, Mary was the first to see him. She was crying, but the rest were still asleep. Mary screamed out in joy, 'My son, my son. He's back.' The light in her eyes began to shine again. As you can imagine, everyone awoke.

"'Yeshua smiled because it seemed we completely forgot our spiritual training and became as children. Everybody awoke and the reactions were amazing. At that moment all of his *brothers,* except for Judas, who was not present, reconnected to the memory of the soul group of 22 and its contract. There had been a tension in the air because of their behavior and each one of them was carrying guilt. When Yeshua walked into the room, all of that completely dispersed. He allowed us to touch him. I later realized that he would not allow me to touch him while we were alone because my physical body would not handle his vibration by itself. With the energy of the soul group together, however, we all touched him easily.

"'His brother's forgiveness came in that moment; it allowed them to feel worthy to continue with the teachings, which were the key to releasing the Anunnaki and their influence from the Garden.'"

"Do you know what it is to have something taken away and then returned?" Rachel looked around at her listeners and smiled to herself, recalling that time. "It was great to see Yeshua again. I was so happy, and Sarah and Binyamin were, too. The room was full of children that morning, laughing and bouncing around. Joy filled the room.

"He was teaching us, without saying a word, what he had taught us his entire life: that death does not exist and that spirit ever continues. The Anunnaki-Sanhedrin were promoting the concept of death as truth, working hard to see to it that the Messiah would never return; but the only way for people to come back to life was upon the return of the Messiah.

"For the people in the room that morning, it was another confirmation that Yeshua had come as the Messiah. We had been grieving him and here he was as if to say, 'Why are you grieving? I told you not long ago that I would always be with you. Remember the Messiah is within you, always, and is the only true, permanent essence.'

"Yeshua sat with all of us and spoke of things to come; He said that each of us must make a choice, to commit to the teachings. In that moment, I made a conscious commitment to follow the ways of the Goddess. In his gentle way, Yeshua offered us the path of grace and said that if anyone in the room wanted to go back to the way of the world, then they should do it now, and not turn back. Every single person in the room was inspired by Yeshua's commitment to the soul contract. Each of his *brothers* committed to continue with the teachings, even though they knew that they might be killed for their choice.

"Later in the afternoon, Father gathered Mary, Miriyam, James, Joseph, and all of the children; he blessed each one of us, touched us, and said, 'Continue with the tradition, and honor the way of Goddess. Know that there is no reason to grieve, for how can you grieve for someone that did not die and will not die?'

"That night was the last night he put me to sleep," Rachel said as a tear rolled down her cheek. "He left sometime during the night. I asked my mother about it once but she did not want to speak of it. I left it alone and it seldom came up again.

"The times to follow were as Yeshua had predicted. Tremendous turmoil and chaos filled Jerusalem and all of Judah. Miriyam wanted to go back to the Qumran/En-gedi area; she wanted to return to the Essene community and some of

Yeshua's *brothers* wanted to as well. Mary wanted to stay in Jerusalem to sit the full seven suns of Shivaah and then, on the 13th sun, return to the tomb.

"Joseph went to Miriyam and Mary after Yeshua had left late Wednesday night, and said to her that he felt it best to leave without sitting Shivaah. Miriyam agreed with him. She knew that Father had not died, but ascended. Mary, however, did not want to leave; she wanted to follow the law, sitting until Friday and then going to the temple.

"Miriyam was concerned for all of us children and for Binyamin in particular. She had seen what had happened to Yeshua, and did not want Binyamin to be in such a negative environment.

"Joseph gave us a donkey to help us reach the Essene community faster. Mary understood why Miriyam wanted to leave. She would sit until Friday and on Sunday, she would leave and go to Nazareth, her hometown.

"Miriyam was pulled in two directions; her heart wanted to stay with Mary to honor the law, but she also felt that she did not need to sit, because Yeshua was not gone. Mary's heart was broken, however, and she was feeling all of the human feelings of her son moving on.

"Something in Miriyam had shifted after seeing Yeshua. He had helped her to create an iron-will focus. She would do whatever she might to take care of the children, and chose to leave that same evening.

SISTERHOOD OF THE DOVE

"Joseph, a couple of Yeshua's *brothers*, and some people from the Essene community, came along with us. We traveled at night because the prayers are said when the sun goes down, and we would not be seen.

"A large group of people stayed with Mary.

"It was of great comfort to travel with Joseph. A group of people returning home late from the temple recognized us and wondered why we were on the road, and where we were going. Joseph gave them a gift of money for a teruma, a contribution for the temple. He suggested that they give to the temple as much as they wanted to and take care of their families with the rest. He was so good with people; he would never put anyone in a compromising position, and he always chose to make people feel that they had the power to do things the right way. Joseph was a businessman, and a good one, but until then, to me, he was just my wealthy uncle who traveled a lot.

"As Essenes, we had promised that our relationship with money would be different. We trusted that we would be provided for sun by sun, and that we did not need to amass anything. Henceforth, we were much freer than most who had money. We never had concerns over belongings and we were never worried about being robbed. It seemed that Joseph must have changed during his time of studying with Yeshua because he seemed free with money, even though he was wealthy.

"We arrived at the Essene community early

Friday morning. They had already heard about what had happened, and were in mourning when we arrived. They were surprised to see us.

"It was good for Miriyam to see Rivka and Baruch again. I believe that she felt pulled to see them, knowing that they would have heard of the trials of our family, and she wanted them to know that she was well.

"Joseph and Miriyam told the Rabbis what had taken place in Jerusalem. They told of Yeshua's resurrection and this made them extremely happy. They wanted to know what Miriyam's plans were, as they knew that being associated with her might bring outside trouble. They did not want the community to be compromised.

"The teachings of Yeshua were not only Essene teachings. Yeshua did not follow the rules of Judaism or any religion; He followed the rules of God and Divine Law. He did not support dogma, but came to expand and add the Holy Spirit. If Yeshua felt that something needed to be done at the sacred times, or on the Sabbath, then he would do it. Nevertheless, Jewish law states that no one is allowed to work at these times. The only time Jewish law does allow for this, is in life-and-death emergencies. Yeshua's intuition was strong and, at times, he felt guided to do things that appeared to break the law.

"Some of the Essene people had dogma lessons of their own; they did not support our path. But Yeshua was loved by the Rabbis, as they remembered who he was and did not allow for any type of revolt. But now that he was gone, and Miriyam was a widow, the community wondered if she would become a burden to them."

Rachel paused and reached for her cup. The storm clouds had drawn closer, moisture filled the air, and she felt within that this was the moment the sisters would choose to be rained on or not.

"Miriyam felt pulled to see Mary. They had been doing everything of the Goddess together and were connected in many ways. Mary was also her link to the womb from which Yeshua had come.

"We stayed in the community for the passing of a moon and slowly it became clear that we must leave, though the community was loving and did not force us out. Leah, especially, did not want Miriyam to leave. She asked her, 'What is going to happen with Rivka and Baruch? This is their home. This is where they are comfortable.'

"Miriyam asked the Rabbis what they thought would be best for Rivka and Baruch, who loved the community and its way of life. Rivka had known it all of her life and Baruch for most of his. Their friends were there. Miriyam gave them the choice to stay with the community or travel with her. She felt they were their own beings and not children anymore. Baruch did well with his studies and they taught him to scribe the Holy Scriptures.

"The Rabbis gave Miriyam permission to leave Binyamin with them, since they wanted to bring him up by their laws, without persecution as well as

Rivka and Baruch. However, she must take Sarah and me with her.

"Miriyam knew that the male patriarchy was leading them to this choice. She knew that they wanted the seed of Yeshua to continue within the Essene community. Miriyam felt that Binyamin must come with her, that he must learn the ways of the Goddess. In seven years time, at age 13, he could make his own choice. My brother and sister, Baruch and Rivka, chose to remain in the Essene community.

"We left: a caravan of 25 to 30 people traveling north. Joseph had been coming and going, as usual, but the Goddess always brought him forth when Miriyam needed him.

"The caravan stopped in Jerusalem on its way north. This was difficult for all of us. While there, we connected with some of Yeshua's *brothers* and sat with them. Jerusalem was in chaos. People were torn; some were grieving, as not everyone had wanted to kill. Once Yeshua died, many people were caught at a fork in the road.

"The quake upon the hill was considered a great miracle and people wondered what they had done. Even many Roman people began to question their dogmatic ways and to believe that Yeshua was King.

"Salome found our caravan on its way through and asked Miriyam to travel with us. Miriyam welcomed her openly and Salome became part of our group.

"At Nazareth, we joined with Mary: a happy reunion, but brief, for Mary's health was failing. It was summertime, and Joseph had brought certain herbs which he offered to nurse her back to health.

"During one of her weaker moments, Mary shared with Miriyam that she had promised the Goddess to travel to Anatolia and build a temple. Since she was uncertain as to whether she would stay in her body, she asked Miriyam to accept the promise to build the temple.

"Miriyam looked into her weary eyes and said with conviction, 'We will both build it.'

"We stayed in Nazareth for the entire summer. It was a hot one. As summer ended, Mary was well enough to travel with us north to Tiberias, where we stayed, even though it was a major Roman community. The Jews there did not belong to the four major sects, though they were wealthy enough. Many of the Jews in Tiberias worked for the Romans. By this time, the Anunnaki-Sanhedrin was looking for us and likely would not expect us to be there.

"As Essenes, we liked Tiberias for its powerful and sacred vortices of energy.

"As Rosh Hashanah approached, we met up with some of Yeshua's *brothers*. They told us that of the 12, 11 were alive. Judas had chosen suicide and some of the 11 had already left Judah to spread the teachings in other countries. They confirmed what we had heard in Jerusalem: that the Anunnaki-Sanhedrin was still looking for them and us. Joseph had already heard this and elected not to tell Miriyam, as he wanted us to have time to heal in a place of repose.

"Miriyam mentioned later that we made it out safely because of Joseph and his influence.

"While in Tiberias, Miriyam received a vision from the Goddess who said, 'Get ready for a long journey. You and Mary will build my temple. You will create a place of worship for the Goddess. You will travel farther north and more and more will unfold as you go.'

"After Miriyam had received the vision, she spoke with Mary, who told her that she had had a dream in which she had heard, 'The time is coming. All of you must strengthen your physical bodies for the journey.'

"Mary and Miriyam told us that we would leave Judah, and our old way of living. Sarah was excited; Binyamin was quiet, and just sat there and listened. I was adamant about staying in my country and continuing the teachings. I would do whatever it took to continue the teachings. I was ready to fight.

"Miriyam explained to me, however, that, in order to grow stronger, we must do so as a family. I knew that I was not old enough to leave; that was my grace. Miriyam said that when I became a young woman, I might choose to return to Judah. She said it broke her heart to leave the country as well. She loved Judah and said, 'Once the Anunnaki had Yeshua crucified, I felt that the soil itself was contaminated and the purity of the land was gone.'"

Rachel wiped the water from her face. It had begun drizzling. "This is as far as we go tonight, children," Rachel said, feeling a healing presence in her throat. "The last time Miriyam and I were together in her dwelling in the south of Gaul, she said, 'It was after his crucifixion and after his ascension that something within me opened up like the dove. Peace grew within me and I realized why I had received the dove's wing at the time of my sacred union with your father. I truly emulated peace after that. The gift the Dove teaches us is that no scar remains when one accepts the Dove into one's being.'"

Rachel paused and allowed Miriyam's words to move into each heart present.

"Imagine, children, healing with no trace of a blemish-- no emotional scars, no physical scars, no mental scars: Complete wholeness." Rachel paused. She looked upon the sisters to see if they embraced the immense love of the Holy Spirit, the immense love that completely heals all wounds.

"The Gateway of the West is your departure point this night. Carved upon its arch is the six-pointed star. As the Servers guide you through this star gate, may your upper and lower natures merge; when this takes place within, the sacred white Dove is called forth.

"Sleep anywhere you choose outside the temple tonight. Move swiftly now, as this drizzle will become a full downpour. RA BA RA."

As the sisters crossed the temple grounds to the

Western Gate, the sky opened. Mother Nature, with a flash of light, a clap of thunder, and a rush of water, cleansed the temple grounds, as all present knew she would.

Soaked to the core and feeling chilled, Rachel made her way to her resting area. She had received the Dove's grace during the last sentences of storytelling, and she knew that her throat would be fine come Ra's first light.

Now in her tent, as she laid her head upon the land, she heard Isis whisper to her, "I cannot let you sleep, my love, not yet anyway. Your Daniel has taken ill this night. He prays to us for assistance and you are called to journey inwardly to him. You will see. He will be fine, but he does need you now. RA BA RA."

Rachel moved her consciousness upon the inner planes to Daniel, served him as the Goddess instructed, and returned to her body to sleep.

CHAPTER 7
THE DOVE RETURNS

It had been a glorious sun in Ephesus. Isis had cleansed the land during the night and all had flowed beautifully during that sun. Rachel received word from the Goddess that Daniel was doing well and that it would be the warmest evening yet for storytelling.

Rachel made her way through the Eastern Arch and was greeted by a dove, which she allowed to land upon her arm. She walked across the grass and took her seat in front, then began to speak. "After she left Judah," Rachel said, "Miriyam ventured to the area in which we sit. It is true that, for generations, people of many cultures have come to this vortex of energy. The energy emitted from the ground here calls those of this particular vibration. Isis called Miriyam and Mary here.

"When we left Tiberias, we walked to Caesarea where Joseph's boat was in the harbor. He had timed our departure for autumn, which was his usual time of departure, and to which we kept so as not to arouse suspicion. Joseph had many connections in that area, as he dealt with the Romans often, and would bring back things from Rome. He would also transport their goods to Rome on his boat. The weather had become cooler and we were uncomfortable because we did not take many things with us. We took only what we needed for the first leg of our journey, which took us past Phoenicia[34] to the north on the way to our final destination, Ephesus. Our group of 12--Joseph, Mary, James, Peter, Salome, Miriyam, Sarah, Binyamin, three others, and I--left on the boat, along with other merchants and the crew.

"This trip would be just like any other of Joseph's merchant dealings. Joseph's trip would take us to Anatolia and he would travel on to Greece, Rome, Gaul, and Spain and return along his route to Caesarea. "We stopped in Phoenicia first. Next, we stopped in Cyprus for seven suns of resting and relaxing. The trip to Anatolia was cold and wearing the poorer, Roman clothing did not help. The garments were not stitched together as tightly as the fabrics we usually wore.

"The waters are always rough during those moons and it was not a fun trip. To make matters worse Mary became ill again. This time it was her heart and lungs. Peter had grown attached to her, partly out of obligation to Yeshua, to whom he had promised the protection of Mary, and did his best to nurse her. I think he felt some remnants of guilt for having denied Yeshua three times upon his capture.

"While resting in Cyprus, Miriyam had a visitation from the Goddess Isis, who took her on the inner realms to a Goddess temple. From there the Goddess told her, 'Not the first place, but the second place that the boat will arrive in Anatolia is the place where you will disembark and build my temple. People will be there to greet you when you arrive.'

"We made our first stop in Anatolia and Joseph wanted us to stay there. He knew people in the area and felt it was closer to Judah. Miriyam told him that it was not the right place for her and asked him if there would be a second stop in Anatolia. He told her that there was a second stop but felt that the first stop was the better place, because it was more populated and had easier access to food.

"Mother communicated her vision, aligning Joseph with the soul contract. He said that there were certain people whom he knew at the second stop, Ephesus, which lay directly across the Great Sea from Athens.

"Our entire trip from Caesarea to Ephesus took almost one full moon. I was nine at the time," Rachel said, drifting off for a moment. "Such a long time ago: During the journey, Miriyam told us stories of her travels around the world with Father.

"Miriyam did not often complain, but during the journey she did say, 'It was much nicer traveling from place to place on the ships of the Hathors. We would glide vast distances in moments without all the ups and downs and feeling seasick much of the time.'

"She reminded us that there were several purposes for their travels. The most significant purpose was for Yeshua to meet and study with the Magi, and teach the groups of people whom the Magi had arranged for him to meet.

"Each time Yeshua met with a Magus, he received an energetic clearing on a cellular level, along with a teaching. In this dimension, one does not truly embody something until one gives it forward. This is one of the reasons the Magi prepared groups of people for Yeshua. As he taught and gave to them, he received the infusion of light, which in turn connected a strand of DNA.

"Miriyam told of a cataclysm that happened to the Garden's entire equilibrium 1000s of festivals ago. She called it the Fall of Atlantis[35]. It was then that the Devic Kingdom receded.

"Miriyam and Yeshua were charged with raising the consciousness to the Garden and one way they did this was to distribute seeds from one area to another; share medicine from one person to another, plant herbs in different areas of the Garden that present and future cultures would need because of the genetic shaking caused by the destruction of

Atlantis. Miriyam, Yeshua, and the entire soul group of 22 were creating balance and unification within the consciousness of the peoples of this Garden so they would no longer feel separate from one another – a result of the genetic shaking.

"The Magi called Yeshua to places in the east, which she called the Land of Buddha[36] and the Land of the Rising Sun[37]. She told us of holy temples built in honor of a special man called Buddha and a mother figure named Quan Yin. She said that to many of these people Buddha was somewhat as Moshe is to the Jews. Miriyam loved traveling to the eastern parts of the world and did so a lot.

"She told us of two places off of the west coast of Spain; she visited the most northerly one only, which she called the Land of the Red Man[38]. As for the southerly Landmass[39], she was guided against visiting for reasons she did not tell us. She shared a drawing of a pyramid located within the southern part of the northern Landmass[40]. They spoke a new language again and it seemed that with each Magus, Father would learn the appropriate tongue to use with the people.

"In the central portion of the northern Landmass[41], she saw a completely different culture again and was fascinated by the music, dance, and dress of the people. She said that she met with a people called the Hopi. She learned the teachings of their katchina spirits, which they prayed to for almost everything, and Miriyam drew one of these images for us.

"The Hathors flew them to the upper part of the northern Landmass[42] and she was shown, from above, the biggest fresh water lakes[43] she had ever seen; the Hathors took her down to merge her energy with the waters of the country. She told us they were very cold. They flew to a place in the mountains[44] where they met with beings that lived under the surface of the Garden's crust. The main reason they connected with these beings was to discuss and learn their ways of living because Yeshua, Miriyam, and the Hathors knew of future quakes to come; they were creating communities independent of government and of the Anunnaki influence. She said that nature was still rebuilding herself from the time of Atlantis, and that it was important to build cities in a way that would not harm the equilibrium of the Garden. Many beings had journeyed there during the Garden's tilt – the Fall of Atlantis.

"The jungles of a place she called the Land of Krishna[45], to the east, brought delight to Miriyam. The Magus called, and, while Yeshua was off, she spent time with an enormous animal with huge ears and a long nose[46]. She said she rode upon one. She even learned of Ganesh, the god connected with this animal. She also learned of a being named Krishna who walked upon the land there, giving teachings of truth; Miriyam likened him to Moshe as well.

"She told us of a place high in the mountains above the Land of Krishna, called Bod[47]. Here she rode upon the back of a wooly animal with a long neck[48]. She drew a picture of it for us to see. Miriyam loved the animal kingdom, and animals felt her love. She was in awe of nature, awed by the rising of each new sun as it came up. She often would say, 'For me every aspect of nature is a miracle, every sun. This is the child-like quality your father and I have. We honored Mother Nature. We always gave gratitude to the elements; gratitude to the rain; gratitude to all.' As Yeshua would take his private time for teaching, Miriyam would gather the animals together and allow them to teach her.

"She told us bits of her adventures in Alba: of meeting the Druids and how similar they were to us in their philosophy. She spoke of stones, great in size, that stood upon end, and of meeting two Ancients whom she called the Magus and the Crone. She spoke more of the magnificent chalice from which she and Yeshua had drunk during their sacred union ceremony.

"The last place she spoke of during our journey to Ephesus, but certainly not the last place she went, was a place upon the far side of the Garden. There they met with a group of beings that had tanned skin and light hair[49]. Mother felt extremely at home with these people as they, too, worked much with the dreamtime. A Magus came forth there to greet Yeshua, and the elder women took Miriyam for teachings in the ways of the dreamtime. She drew another animal unlike we had ever seen before. It had long, strong back legs, upon which it stood erect, and a small pouch upon its front for carrying its offspring. It hopped around instead of walking[50].

"During nights on the boat I would listen in on conversations between Miriyam and James. On one of those nights I heard them speaking of Yeshua's *brothers* and their part in the soul contract. The two of them went through the teachings, both positive and negative, that each was to teach the world. I absorbed them that night, and, later, when I was older, I asked Miriyam to help me remember what James had said of himself and his 11 other *brothers.*

"Uncle James went through it something like this that night on the boat.

"'The soul contract of 22 called for 12 of us to radiate specific teachings to the peoples of this Garden. Each of us chose our name, as you did, with a specific meaning and purpose for us to carry out our missions. Yeshua invoked our memories and our call to service after he gathered each of us.

"'Simon, who later was given the name Peter by Yeshua, came to mirror the lesson of initiative. His name, Simon, means *listening,* and, while expressing himself in a balanced way, he represented the ability to listen to God's initiative. He was as immovable in his beliefs as the name Peter, which means *stone* or *rock*, suggests.

"'Peter was asked to initiate the energy of denial during Yeshua's trial, giving the perception that he was not rock solid in his beliefs, was self-involved, and easily changed his mind.

"'It may be easy for us to mistake Peter's denial

of Yeshua as him not following God's initiative, when really it is what the Lord had asked of him. Yeshua desired the teachings continued and all of us, his *brothers,* would have been crucified beside him, had we not followed his desire.

"'Simon, who came from Canaan, mirrored the lesson of dependability. Simon belonged to the sect of the Zealots, who greatly resisted the Roman government. As I mentioned a moment ago, Simon means *listening*, but it may also mean *hearkening.*'

"'Simon's energy, while expressed in a balanced way, asked people to contemplate, 'Upon whom do I depend for food, for money, for shelter? Do I depend upon God to provide for me, or do I depend upon governments?'

"'When directed to express in an imbalanced way, Simon believed in fighting governments, materialism, security, acquisition, and wealth. While expressing balance, he hearkened, or gave heed, to the call of the Lord and depended upon Him with the utmost faith.

"'I came to mirror the lesson of flexibility. When my expression is balanced, I teach those around me to yield their personalities to the Will of God. When my expression is imbalanced, I mirror, as my name, James, suggests, how people confuse themselves by having many identifications and personalities, all believing different things.

"'Andrew incarnated to mirror the lesson of nurturance to the peoples of this Garden. He, indeed, was like a mother to all of us. He expressed balance through modeling how a man, the meaning of the name *Andrew* being *man,* merged with his feminine nature. Andrew genuinely cared for those around him.

"'Andrew expressed his imbalance each time we traveled. He loved the idea of a home and preparing a sacred space. Yeshua taught that God resides in each heart. Andrew, upon more than one occasion, dug deeply to maintain his connection to home. When Yeshua taught of the temple of God, he was usually speaking of a human being's physical body, which houses the soul and spirit. Andrew incarnated to awaken the spirit within people to care for their temples – their physical bodies - and to nurture them as a mother nurtures her child.

"'John, brother of James, came to mirror the lesson of courage. John's name means *God is gracious.* As a balanced expression, John taught the graciousness of God's merciful and compassionate heart.

"'John's expression of pride, boasting, and taking glory for himself rather than giving glory to our Lord mirrored to people that they had disconnected from their hearts. Courage may be motivated by fear or faith.

"'Philip came to mirror the lesson of organization. To many people, a horse represents power. Philip's name means *friend of horses.* Do you recall how many questions he would ask, always wanting to know more and enquiring about this and that? He came to teach of the power of the mind. Authentic intention is a thought aligned with spirit, and, thus, that thought truly has the power to manifest into something desirable. With balanced expression, Philip organized his thoughts, which aligned his mind with spirit and used this power to create. Yeshua taught, 'As a man thinketh in his heart, so shall he be'. This was Philip's favorite teaching.

"'When imbalanced, Philip's disorganized mind would allow this power to turn on him, and the resulting energy was unfriendly.

"'Bartholomew came to mirror the lesson of balance. It was evident early that he would lead many to the Lord. Like his name, meaning *furrowed,* he understood what was beneath the surface. While aligned, Bartholomew, or Nathaniel, as some called him, gave us the gift of true balance, going under the surface and preparing us for something new.

"'When spirit desired his expression as imbalanced, however, he would become cutting, overbearing, manipulative in a negative way, and responded to others with little tact. One always knew when Bartholomew's expression was out of alignment, because he buried his usual way of clarity, humor, and charm deep within himself.

"'Thomas incarnated to mirror the lesson of transformation. With balanced expression, Thomas was probably the most intuitive of us all. His abilities allowed him to commune with spirit readily. Through his gift of healing, Thomas saw into others and was possibly the best at it of the 12. Yeshua reminded each of us of the healer within. Thomas transformed lives much the way Yeshua performed physical *miracles.*

"'Thomas expressed doubt, lack of faith, and suspicion when he was directed to express his energy in an imbalanced way.

"'James, brother of John, came to mirror the lesson of philosophy. James loved travel and loved to express his opinion, which at times was honest to a fault. Therefore, the life of traveling came naturally to James, and the message that the soul group came to deliver flowed easily from him. One meaning of the name James is *holder of the heel,* and, when asked to express himself from a state of imbalance, he held onto an ideal so tightly that he would lose all perspective. His sense of justice was great and wonderfully put to use when expressed through his philosophical thought. Yet, if his steadfast ways locked onto a narrow-minded project or line of thought, then he would not think at all of the price he and those close to him might pay for his actions.

"'Brother Matthew incarnated to mirror the lesson of responsibility. Give him a task to do, and if he accepted, then there was no better person of the 12 to accomplish it. His name means *gift of God.* While expressing himself from this place of alignment with the Lord, he offered people the opportunity to give. He was employed as a tax collector, prompted by Spirit into this role so that people might have the opportunity to give with love rather than resentment. Yes, the Anunnaki had its influence over the country of which one was taxed, but, if the people accepted the government they chose, rather than falling victim to it, then it would be much better for them.

"'Matthew expressed imbalance as being one of many faces: acting one way while believing another, creating power struggles amongst people, or working excessively.

"'Thaddaeus birthed himself to mirror the lesson of community. His balanced expression called him to share with others how to unite and commune with their hearts; Thaddaeus means *heart*. His energy taught that if one did not connect with one's own heart, then one would not connect with the global heart.

"'When Thaddaeus was asked to express himself in an imbalanced way, he was rude and tactless. At other times he expressed uncertainty and looked toward his own personal gain rather than asserting his views, which brought him to changing his mind to fit in and belong with the crowd.

"'Yeshua's and my cousin, Judas Iscariot, brings this transmission to completion. He incarnated to mirror the lesson of vision. Long before Judas responded to Spirit's call to offer Yeshua to the Anunnaki-Sanhedrin, he already had feelings of jealousy and competition. Yeshua loved Judas dearly and often reminded him not to compare. Later when Yeshua opened Judas's memory and the vision of the soul contract that called for him to offer Yeshua to the Anunnaki, Judas became mentally unstable.

"'You see, Judah's conscious memory held only the view of the soul group returning as the Messiah consciousness. When Yeshua unlocked for him the path that this Garden had chosen to unfold, he did not embrace it. He did not have the emotional or mental support of the human collective consciousness to hold the vision in a balanced way. Because of this, he did not want to follow the Plan. He wanted to be favored as Yeshua was. In the end, he did not embrace self-forgiveness. Committing suicide was not part of the vision, his death was; but not by suicide. The vision Judas saw not only held with it the offering of Yeshua but also had the end of his own physical body. The soul contract held in it that Judas would find salvation in death similar to Yeshua as each was fulfilling their part. Judas turned away his faith, let go of the vision, and opted for another path. He now lives in further torment and it grieves us all because he represented symbolically the 12th strand of the DNA. Each brother stepped forward in unique order as Yeshua collected around him the outer manifestation of one's inner DNA. With Judas joining last, he symbolized the 12th strand. By his free will act of disconnecting, the entire symbolism of what we put together as the soul group of 22 became out of balance. Humanity, for a moment, lost its reflection of the 12th strand. A short time later, Yeshua appeared before a Roman named Paul, and called forth the memory within him of his contract of the soul group of 22.

"'Shortly after Yeshua met the 12th Magus he was called into the Sinai. There he confronted his inner demons for 40 suns with the help of an Anunnaki warrior. Judas's overwhelming choice of free will was aided by the collective consciousness in that we were unwilling to face our own inner demons. This manifested as Judas going mad and prematurely ending his life.

"'In the expression of balance, Judas carried himself with playfulness, strength, laughter, vision, and foresight, as well as the willingness to speak with anyone about anything. His name means *praised* and, because of his love and commitment, he should be praised for following through on the soul contract to pierce the shadow veil of the Anunnaki. You and I both know that the meaning of the number 30 is *dedication* and this is how many pieces of silver Judas arranged to be paid; even in this he chose silver because of its significance to the feminine. Even though his insides were tearing apart in inner conflict, he still sent forth a message to the Anunnaki that he was dedicated to the Dove.'"

Rachel looked upon her sisters, smiling. She saw in the faces of many that they had harshly judged Yeshua's *brothers*. She felt an inner contentment as they absorbed a new view of the past within themselves. She took a sip of water from her cup and continued when she felt they were ready.

"That night we recalled just how much detail we had written into the soul contract." Rachel stood, stretched, and invited all to join her and take in a deep breath. When they had settled back in, Rachel resumed her story.

"When we arrived in the harbor outside of Ephesus, Joseph was surprised that his friends were there, waiting for him, as he had sent no word ahead that we were coming. Somehow, his friends knew that we would be there and had brought with them a full group of women.

"Joseph's friend was a wealthy man who lived in the area. He had six daughters who immediately took us to their home; they opened their arms to us and invited us to stay as long as we were guided. They had heard about Yeshua. They knew him, they loved him, and they felt sad about the crucifixion. They embraced us as their own.

"At this time Mary was in and out of her body. Her health was failing, the journey had taken its toll upon her, and the level of human suffering she felt for the loss of her son was immense. Being with the children, especially Binyamin, really brightened her up.

"That winter was a cold one. Miriyam, in her dreamtime, had received a strong prompting to go for three suns' time to the site where the temple would be erected. In the dream, she was instructed to tell no one of her intentions to leave. She was only to tell our hostess, Zurka, that she would travel. She was to take enough cheese, oil, milk, and water for three suns.

"Zurka, who herself had a strong Goddess connection and was a wise being, said to Miriyam, 'May the Goddess be with you.' Zurka winked at her with her left eye. Miriyam smiled and thought to herself, 'How can you keep anything a secret? We are all Goddesses!' Then Miriyam heard an inner chuckle that said, 'It does not matter what anybody knows inside. It is about learning how people disperse energy with their vocal cords: It is about learning how people speak about certain things before they have laid their plans and brought them into the blueprint of this dimension. When people speak of these things, the energy dissipates and manifestation is more difficult to obtain.' Miriyam understood that keeping it a secret from people was not keeping it a secret from others, but rather, keeping it contained within the self so that the energy would build, strengthen, and take root. It was about the will to create the energy within, to become one with it, and henceforth to create the reserve of energy and the focus of energy to bring forth the endurance to accomplish each task.

"Zurka said, 'I have prepared a donkey outside, and there is a whole basket of provisions ready for you.'

"Mother told her that she did not need it, but Zurka insisted, 'The basket is there. Everything you need is in it. There are also some blankets for you. I shall have one of my women and one of my boys go with you.'

"Miriyam told her that she must do it alone and Zurka, loving mother that she was, insisted, 'You don't understand. There are all kinds of forces out there.'

"Isis looked through Miriyam's eyes as she repeated, 'I must do it alone.'

"Zurka yielded her caretaking ways, remembered the Goddess, and returned to center, saying in a tone full of faith, 'Fine.'

"The two hugged, and Miriyam left. Outside she started walking and the donkey followed her with all of the provisions. It was cold, and she did not know where to go. She asked the Goddess to show her the way. She felt 15 again. She implored me to remember this: "Even though you will reach a level of growth where you come from the awareness of Spirit, your emotions, mind, and soul still may be battered in this dimension. As much as I have come from a place of Spirit throughout my life, being detached from the human experience is a continual challenge to maintain. Detachment must be renewed with each sun. One may not grow comfortable by saying, 'I have learned this, I do not need to exercise it.' One must continually maintain the lesson of detachment, just as one must continually give a plant water and sunlight. Anyone who achieves full surrender will go through periods of trial, and periods of humility to be connected again, to be hurting again so they may remember the joy of this physical dimension.'

"Miriyam sat upon the side of the road with the

donkey not far away. She had called upon the Goddess and her response from the Goddess came as a flock of white doves, circling above her head. Several landed upon the donkey's back.

"Miriyam mounted the donkey and said to the Goddess, 'Lead me to where I must go.' With the assistance of the doves and the donkey, she reached a clearing in two suns. There were rain and cold upon the second sun and Miriyam felt pushed by the elements to choose to move forward or turn back. Just when she felt the journey growing too difficult, she reached the clearing, and she knew that the Goddess and the animals had led her to the space for the temple. The Goddess blessed the site with a magnificent rainbow parting the clouds. The rainbow touched the spot where the altar is now, at the center of this temple, where once there were only crumbled stone ruins.

"Miriyam whispered, 'I have come home!' Not to some physical place but to the end of her planning and training to what was finally about to blossom. She knew that the time was right to pass on the harvest of all the teachings she had learned on her journey with the Goddess.

"Miriyam leaned forward and whispered into the donkey's ear jokingly, 'Do you remember the journey back?' As she left, an old woman appeared a short distance down the path, dressed all in black; as Mother came alongside her, they looked into each other's eyes; the woman's face was full of open sores. She continued to look into Miriyam's eyes and Miriyam saw that she had the same gray amber eyes as Yeshua. Miriyam, continuing to look into her eyes, felt tears of love rolling down her cheeks. She climbed from the donkey and hugged the old woman, who returned her hug and said, as they released their embrace, 'Welcome home--I've been waiting.'

"Miriyam returned to the donkey and left the basket of food with the old woman. The return home felt much shorter to her. The weather continued to improve and Miriyam felt lighter. Excitement and a sense of direction returned to her. On Friday, Miriyam returned to the home of Zurka and immediately spoke to Mary. She told her that the Goddess had prepared a wonderful space for her temple and that Mary's vision would soon manifest.

"We honored the Sabbath, and on Sunday we left to see and to honor the site. The group that left for the temple site included Mary, Miriyam, Joseph, Peter, James, Salome, Sarah, Binyamin, the six daughters of Zurka, and me.

"We arrived two suns later, full of anticipation, which quickly turned to joy and excitement as Miriyam shared the Goddess's plans for the temple's design. During that night, some of the people received guidance about returning in the morning; The children, however, would stay. Mary and Salome, also, chose to stay. Joseph, Peter, James, and the six daughters of Zurka returned home.

"See what Mary and Miriyam created with the

support of the Goddess. They had no money, they had just entered a new country, and the Goddess wanted a temple erected, the circumference of the Great Pyramid in Egypt. We spent those first suns in prayer, asking the Goddess to provide the materials for the temple, and the people to serve her with physical labor.

"The Goddess answered our prayers when Joseph returned with Zurka's husband, who greatly supported the ways of the Goddess had agreed to aid in the building of the temple. Joseph himself said that he would contribute finances and gather things during his travels that the Goddess inspired him to bring to the temple. We received tremendous support from the local community in the building of the temple as well.

"Zurka's husband purchased the finest materials available to him, and Joseph brought things from his travels. What you see is the result.

"During that time, we built other, smaller dwellings to live in. We also prepared a garden of foods to nurture us.

"After Yeshua left, our diets changed; we ate much more simply, without the flesh of animals. We ate more fruits and nuts, grains and vegetables, with a small amount of dairy. Through the first couple of festivals, a lot of the food was brought to us.

"People worked continually. The weather was constantly changing, from cold, to warm and sunny. The temple itself took us 18 moons to complete.

The lodgings around the community continued being built after that time, as well as the food garden and the grounds, including the herb garden full of herbs from around the world. We, the sisters, are charged with knowing a variety of different herbs, how to grow them and how each herb is used.

"You will learn here how to lay your hands upon people and heal them in a sun. When Yeshua was alive the healings were done out in the open, but because of the choices we made, and of what happened to him, the Goddess does not want healings to happen this way anymore. After Yeshua left the physical plane, the Garden went through much change. People no longer traveled on the flying ships and no longer teleported; the Goddess requested this so as to draw as little attention to the temple as possible. The Goddess does not want us to create turbulence, in which people will end up following an outer, physical being. She has asked that we disguise the healings behind the plants, the waters, and the other elements of the land. We must awaken the people to honor the Garden, through honoring the energy of the Goddess. We use the energies within this Garden and her healing properties, appealing to people's limited consciousness with herbs, which are tangible. By being with us, many of the people created emotional clearing and healing as well. Their hearts opened, and they transcended much of the density in the areas of judgment and skepticism.

"Of the many who experienced and witnessed

healings, some of them wanted to study the science of herbs so that they might help others. We have classes upon the temple grounds.

"I once asked Miriyam if she performed miracles and she said, 'To me the erecting of the temple in that short period of time was a miracle. At times, during the building process, many accidents might have occurred, but by clearing certain energies, with the techniques you shall learn in your Goddess training, those accidents did not occur. How do you suppose we erected those stone columns? Rachel, do you believe that I lifted those stones on my own? You will learn how to use the magnetic forces to move matter as the ancients did, as the Egyptians did when they erected the Great Pyramid. Listen to me, curious one; being with your father made the reality of miracles constant and ordinary. Together we grew far above the idea of differentiating the creation of energy to dense up as a miracle. The awareness you will learn through the teachings is to look at everything as a miracle. To differentiate any deed to be better than another, an idea of comparison and judgment is created.'

"I do remember," Rachel smiled, "waking in the mornings and seeing the stones piled upon one another and wondering along with everyone else how they got there. A small group would stay up during the night moving them into position. We were not allowed to tell anyone of this and the members of the community were often amazed and left with the awareness that we were doing something special and magical in the building of this Goddess temple.

"We completed the temple upon the summer solstice, one moon before the Alignment of Sirius and the Festival time. Miriyam rose early that sun and went to check on the water-path that led from the river to the temple. It was the first time that the water would enter the altar in a ceremonial way. The altar had been examined prior and then drained. Miriyam spoke her blessing to the Goddess and was pleasantly surprised when she opened her eyes to see the Crone standing beside her, smiling. 'You are to be the first to enter the temple, my dear. Once in there, sing the song of the Dove and call them forth to prepare the space for the other 12 *sisters*. They shall enter from the Gateway of the East.' The Crone anointed Miriyam, embraced her, and gave her a gentle shove.

"Thirteen sisters were present for that first ceremony and, right away, we felt that neither Mary nor Miriyam stood above any of us. We were all sisters and we were all of different ages. I was the youngest, a child of about 10. Mary, who had completed her part of the soul contract, was the eldest. Binyamin stayed with the men. No male form was present in the temple that day. Permission for boys to enter the temple occurred shortly after.

"There would be no individual titles in this temple; everyone would be acknowledged for the unique gift of their presence, which was immeasurable." Rachel moved her hands to her heart and as she did so, a stirring and fluttering of dove wings was heard around the garden.

"More people came as time went on and families joined the community. The openness of the people who came was wonderful, and rarely did we sense judgment from them. The Goddess truly brought forth the people whom she wanted to experience her temple and the temple grounds. From time to time, merchants would pass by, and, upon other occasions, the Goddess brought Roman people. It was apparent to us that only people who were ready for the energy of the Goddess were drawn to the temple grounds.

"Slowly, over the next six festivals, word spread over a great distance. People and families came for healings and teachings. One must belong to the Sisterhood to enter the temple, except for this once a festival, but anyone might be involved in the community.

"Every now and then people would come from Judah. There were those amidst the turbulence in Judah who had chosen to follow the teachings of Yeshua, so the Goddess directed them our way. People in Judah who chose to follow Yeshua's teachings were being ridiculed and, worse, they were being killed.

"Miriyam had friends whom she met during her travels with Yeshua, who came to visit, and some of them joined the Sisterhood. Many times the three Druid women present at Miriyam and Yeshua's sacred union came and stayed with us. They would travel back and forth with Joseph. At times, they would stay for a half moon and once they even stayed for six moons.

"Zurka had a sister who lived in Jerusalem with her family. Joseph would bring her over for visits. She would bring news of what was happening in Judah and what was happening in, and to, the different sects. Many people had turned to materialism and Jerusalem had become the stronghold of the Anunnaki.

"Upon several occasions, Zurka's sister brought her son Daniel along. Within a couple festivals of meeting Daniel, he and I fell in love, and, when I was 17, Miriyam gave her blessing to our union. I shall speak more later of Daniel and me.

"Once in a while, we met some of Yeshua's *brothers*, who had flown from Judah because of the rule of the Anunnaki-Sanhedrin. It was always good to see them; we had wonderful times listening to their stories of inspiring people to merge with the Holy Spirit.

"When Sarah turned 14, she informed Miriyam that it was time for her to leave. She knew what she would do and where she would go. Miriyam had known for some time that Sarah would return to the place of her conception and told Sarah that she would leave with the three Druid sisters the next time they came on the boats with Joseph. That happened a short while later. I did not see Sarah again until the time of my sacred union with Daniel.

"Miriyam and Binyamin kept in touch with

Sarah upon the inner plane, as Miriyam had done with Yeshua in the early times. I knew how to do this, but at that time, I preferred not to use this gift often. I was unaware of it at the time and know now that I needed to remain rooted to the land for the mission that I came to serve as part of the soul group of 22.

"Returning now to my sacred union with Daniel: I was in my late teens when he proposed to me. We were united upon the temple grounds. People came from all over to celebrate us. Joseph brought Sarah, the three Druid women, and others. The Crone did not come to our ceremony, but she did visit me in a dream three nights before. She blessed me and prepared me for the departure of Miriyam, saying, 'After Miriyam leaves, the temple will go through changes; the land will shift ever so slightly and a new vibration will come forth. You are here charged with the task of stabilizing this energy. One of the ways you will do this is by bringing forth children. The sisters need, not a leader, but a guide. Your charge is to be that loving guide in service to the Goddess.' At that point I realized that Miriyam had never really been the head of the Sisterhood. The head always had been, and would remain, the Crone. She had taken care of this land long before any of us had arrived, and would take care of it long after we were all gone. From that time forth, in my awareness, the Crone was the head.

"I went to Miriyam and asked her if she would

leave after my sacred union ceremony. She hugged me, told me she loved me, and said yes. She reminded me of my conception; saying that the way things are conceived in this dimension has a lot to do with their outcome. She reminded me that I was conceived after Yeshua had aided her in releasing fear. This meant that I was the one to carry on the seed of Yeshua. And when I say *the one*, I am speaking from the place of the soul group of 22. Binyamin went on to have children, but he was not part of that soul group. The Goddess had other plans for his descendants. The soul contract called for Yeshua's seed, as it relates to the soul group, to pass through the female, not the male. She told me that I would have children and maintain the energy of the Goddess within my heart.

"The Goddess had appeared to her saying that her stay at the temple was growing short. The Goddess told her that it was time for her to go and spread the teachings."

Rachel stopped and took in some water; looking around, she gave a huge smile, shifting the vibration, and continued, "My sacred union ceremony combined the ways of the Goddess with traditional Judaism.

"Shortly following our ceremony, Zurka, whom I love dearly, hinted to Miriyam that she was available if mothering was needed in her absence; Miriyam and I were content with that.

"Mary felt at home in Ephesus and she chose to stay; she loved the temple and knew she would lay down her body in this area when the time came. She had entered a place in her life where she spent more and more time in meditation and communion with God. She at times taught the young ones, as she always loved doing that. She ate and drank little."

Tears rolled down Rachel's cheeks. "Mary left her body just a few festivals ago. It was a good day. The sun shone and the doves circled her dwelling in the hills. You may feel her energy as it moves and inspires throughout the temple grounds."

Rachel took a moment to reflect upon the physical absence of Mary. "Binyamin came to us during that time as well, and said that he would go with Miriyam. He had long felt protective over her, and I believe this was part of his reasoning for making the journey which brought us here. He was also growing restless with the temple way of life, and wanted to explore more of the Garden. Binyamin had had his own dream around the time when I had mine, in which he was guided to leave. When he mentioned that he would leave with Miriyam, she jokingly said, 'You may not come.'

"He became somewhat defensive and retorted, 'What do you mean I may not come? Yes, I may, and I shall.'

"'Why would you want to come?' Miriyam said in jest.

"'I get messages, too, you know!'

"'Do you?' Miriyam nudged some more.

"'Why, don't you know I get messages?' Binyamin said, getting more upset.

"Miriyam reached out and pulled him to her, saying that she would be honored for him to join. I saw that her heart was happy for his choice.

"When it came time for Miriyam and the others to leave, she told me that the soul group had established in Ephesus what we had not yet established in the Holy Temple of Jerusalem: the consciousness of humans had accepted the return of the Dove. We both knew there was a lot still to unfold in the soul contract, but in that moment, we reflected upon the physical beauty of the temple; we reflected upon all of the pain Miriyam had endured and healed to see the Sisterhood of the Dove manifest. We knew that, at any moment, the Garden might quake and the temple might tumble to the ground, but it mattered not to Miriyam, because the temple of the Goddess was forever etched into the heart of the Garden and her peoples would find it when they were ready.

"The Crone interrupted that conversation, which took place at night under the starry sky at the edge of the river. She said nothing to Miriyam or to me, but squeezed Miriyam so tightly that I thought Miriyam would stop breathing. She left as swiftly as she had come, and Miriyam and I retired for the evening without a word.

"The next morning the community watched as Miriyam, Sarah, Binyamin, Salome, the six daughters of Zurka, and the three Druid women left the temple grounds to join Joseph at the harbor. I did not travel to the shore to see them off; instead I went to the temple, knelt by the altar, and prayed to the Goddess for their safe passage."

Rachel paused for breath, then said, "Storytelling concludes for this night, children. The Servers will guide you through the Gateway of the Northwest with its symbol of the chalice. The chalice represents the feminine. In our human forms, we are constantly given the choice to fill our vessels with attachments, or with divine spirit. Tonight, as you move through the arch, may you leave behind your attachment to a personal identity, and may you be open to the divine love of the Goddess.

"Until dusk is upon us once more, my beloved sisters, I remind you to say prayers for yourselves, for others, and for our beloved Garden. I remind you to invoke Isis before going to sleep this night, and I say to you that you are never alone; the Goddess is always with you. RA BA RA."

CHAPTER 8
SECRET SOCIETIES

The evening was perfectly clear, without a cloud in the sky. The Garden and Sirius were making their rotations in the universe and nearing the time of the Alignment. Soon the moon would set, and, for the briefest of moments, the energy of unconditional love would stream forth from Sirius. Temples all over the Garden's surface would activate their sacred centers one by one as the Garden gradually spun through space. Each temple was a musical vibration in the sound of Her life. A grid of light would spread from temple to temple, starting in the Far East. It would progress to Ephesus, and move on through Britain, out across the great waters off of the west coast of Eire[51] to the two huge landmasses, of which Miriyam spoke, before progressing back to where it started.

Rachel arrived late this evening. She had been in deep meditation during the rest period, and had taken some extra time to anchor herself into her body. As she took her seat, a young child came to her with a gift. Rachel accepted it, kissed the child upon both cheeks, and placed the gift upon her little table.

"Seven nights ago I opened our story in the middle," she said. "Tonight, we shall close the story in the middle.

"By this time all of the members of my birth family had left to follow their paths which the Goddess had mapped out for them.

"Ten festivals would pass before Joseph took Daniel, me, and our two youngest children to visit Miriyam in Gaul. Our two older children stayed in Ephesus with Zurka. During the trip, Miriyam shared more of her travels and what she did after she left Ephesus and the temple grounds.

"When her journey began, Miriyam didn't know she would eventually settle in Gaul. All she knew was that the Goddess would reveal each step to her when she must know. One thing became evident, however; she would not be alone. Several people were called to travel with her.

"Greece was the first stop, where they came across some of Yeshua's *brothers*, who had been spreading the teachings. In Greece, they also found Lazarus and his two sisters, Martha and Mary, and their families. Lazarus had accepted a second life from Yeshua at an earlier time, which inspired people to see that death was not permanent. Miriyam said, 'We were all happy to see them and they were happy to see us. This is the beautiful thing about soul family. Whether or not we are blood, we are always connected, no matter where we have been, or how long it has been since we have seen each other.'

"They had heard of the temple in Ephesus and inquired as to what Miriyam was doing and where she was headed. Miriyam told them that she was traveling with Joseph and would be stopping along the way as she was prompted. The Goddess would lead her to the next place she would settle down. They stayed for a while with Lazarus and his family before the Goddess urged her on to Rome.

"Soon after arriving, Miriyam learned from Joseph that three members of the Anunnaki-Sanhedrin, who were part of Yeshua's sentencing, were there; having been brought to Rome for imprisonment. It was Jewish custom to judge lawbreakers in Judah if they had broken Roman law. However, if the Sanhedrin were found guilty of breaking the law, then they would be tried in Rome, to avoid an uprising or revolt within the country.

"Miriyam initially thought, 'Good! They deserve it,' but instantly regretted it. She knew that the Goddess way was of forgiveness and she had not yet found it within herself. She prayed for healing between herself and these men, and was directed to speak with Joseph about it.

"She asked him if he would speak to the praetor who governed that section in Rome, but he protested. He felt that they deserved punishment, but after seeing the look in Miriyam's eyes, he recalled her vows and yielded, using his influence to create a meeting with the praetor.

"As they entered, the praetor recognized Joseph and asked him why they had come. Joseph told him that they had come to ask for the freedom of the three Sanhedrin Priests.

"The praetor said, 'It will not be done,' to which Joseph replied, 'I believe you have the power to free them.' Miriyam remained quiet.

"As the conversation finished and they prepared to be dismissed, Miriyam spoke up, looking deep into the eyes of the praetor. 'Do you have a daughter who is very ill?'

"The praetor replied, 'Yes, I do. How do you know?' Miriyam said that God had told her, and then asked to see his daughter. The praetor took Joseph and Miriyam to his home.

"Miriyam spent the night with his daughter, using herbs and her gift of healing. The next morning, the girl awoke as if she had never been ill. The praetor and his wife thanked Miriyam and said, 'Go on your way, and everything will be fine.'

"As they left, Miriyam asked Joseph, 'He will let them go, won't he?'

"Joseph placed his hand in hers. 'Yes, he will.'

"Joseph and Miriyam were well out of sight

when he released the men, so that it would not look like the praetor had been influenced by anyone regarding this choice; he must maintain his power before the Roman people.

"This was a great lesson for Miriyam about forgiveness; for a brief moment, she had become the wife, the widow, and the victim of others' choices. Yeshua had told her that she would love all of God's children as she did her own. Now the Goddess had brought the three men upon her path to offer her the experience of forgiveness and unity.

"'Rachel,' she said to me, 'at each sun you must awaken to a completely new Garden. Upon rising, one may not maintain the same attitudes from the sun before. It matters not how long one has studied the teachings or how long one has prayed. Each sun the dust of life collects upon people as it collects upon a table. As one daily cleans the table of that dust so must one clean oneself each moment while one is in this Garden. Every word that one utters, every exhalation, and each step one takes creates an energetic reaction. This was a wonderful awakening for me; here I was working and being with the Goddess for so long, being in wonderful companionship, seeing the Divine in people and recognizing how a thought the size of a pinhead might come in and disperse it all.'

"I wondered if Miriyam was being too hard on herself. I would have thought the same and probably a lot more. Yet, she was exquisite, not judging herself for her thoughts and her feelings.

She had looked deep inside at a point of shadow within herself and brought forth the light of healing.

"'Why did you heal his daughter?' I asked her, 'and how did you know you would heal yourself this way?'

"'I did not heal his daughter,' Miriyam said, responding to my question. 'The Goddess healed his child to get to her father's heart, and mine. When one is healed, all are healed. I did not go into that room to heal his daughter; I went to free the three Sanhedrin Priests. The Goddess directed my words and actions while I was with the praetor. My personal healing came later, with the freeing of the Priests.'

"After Rome came Marseille, Gaul, where she would settle, 18 moons later.

"The Goddess reminded her of the Sacred Rose Line within the Garden, and told her of another sacred energetic Line that continues from the Rose Line at a certain point in Gaul. The Goddess recommended that Miriyam walk this Line or pathway. Miriyam did not question, preparing herself for the journey, which would largely be on foot.

"Mother, James, Binyamin, Salome, and a few others took a boat to the beginning of the energetic Line[52]. Some of the people who had been traveling with Mother stayed in Marseille.

"As he walked the Line, James received a message from the Goddess to stay and teach. The rest wished him well and departed[53].

"With the walk complete, the energetic seeds planted, and the contract fulfilled for that area of the Garden, they returned to Marseille, where Binyamin, who was now in his late teens, was united with his love. I was not called to attend.

"During her time in Marseille, Miriyam saw a lot of movement with the teachings of Yeshua, in many different places. Many of the people were practicing them in secret. Several secret societies honored the teachings in the underground, out of the public eye.

"Miriyam took an exceptionally long time to walk that Sacred Line. I am left with only hints of other conversations and an awareness from my meditations that she passed on teachings of the Goddess ways and helped to create the secret societies."

Rachel paused, reflecting on Miriyam's life of service to the Goddess. "I am almost 50. I have been here at this temple for almost 40 festivals. Many have traveled through its gateways. Many have entered the Sisterhood and ventured forth with the teachings they learned here. Maybe some of you will move to these grounds after..." Rachel's voice faded and she did not finish her thought.

"Are you all right, Ima?" asked a woman in the front row, reaching out to touch Rachel's foot.

"I am, sweetie," Rachel responded, feeling nostalgic. "When the cord was cut and we separated from our birth mothers, we forged individual lives calling forth the lessons of suffering through the illusion of separation. In the morning, you will reconnect yourself to the Goddess Isis. The light of Sirius will energize the large, black stone atop the altar in the center of the pool. You will bathe in starlight, drink the healing waters from the pool, and recall that each of you entered as individuals and only One will exit.

"You will sleep little tonight. You will rise early, and meditate before entering the temple garden. Be here well before sunrise tomorrow morning. Upon entering the temple, you will remain in silence until the sphere of Ra has crested the horizon. At such time, instructions will be given.

"As of last night you have merged with each Gateway of the temple. Energetically you were infused with the symbol of each Gateway as you moved through its arch. Tonight you will choose the Gateway from which to depart. In making your choice, I suggest you take a moment to contemplate how the Goddess is asking you to manifest your path of service. The symbol atop each arch is a school of teaching here at the Sisterhood. You are required to study the teachings of each symbol, but the way you will teach – the energy that you will transmit while teaching – will be infused by the Gateway of your choice as you leave here tonight.

"Know that each of you is in my heart. RA BA RA."

CHAPTER 9
WELCOMING THE DOVE

Rachel sat upon the grass in the temple garden, communing with Isis. She did not return to her rest area, as Isis had asked her to remain. It was a beautifully warm night; the moonlight reached the temple periodically through the clouds of Nut's overcast sky. At midnight, Rachel felt the Crone enter the temple. She opened her eyes and, peering through the darkness, saw her making her way toward her. Rachel wondered what had called her to the temple garden. She rarely came before an initiation. In fact, Rachel knew of only three other times in which she had come upon a night such as this: the first and last times Miriyam gave the initiations, and the first time Rachel had given the initiations.

Rachel felt the Crone smile through the darkness. The clouds covering the moon faded and Rachel watched as she walked over to the altar stone and placed her hand upon it. She spoke a word unfamiliar to Rachel and her hand moved into the stone as if it were liquid. In the moonlight Rachel saw little, but she did see the Crone withdraw something from the altar stone.

She turned and walked to Rachel. Lifting and turning Rachel's left hand; she placed the object in her palm and closed her fingers tightly, then spoke. "Of the soul group of 22, only three inhabit human from now: you, your sister Sarah, and Joseph."

Rachel's eyes welled up with tears. The Crone tenderly wiped Rachel's eyes with her sleeve. "There will be time to feel your feelings. For now, you must listen to what I have to say. A few moments ago Miriyam graduated her physical form. She will visit you shortly. You have served the Dove well and tonight was the last time you will tell this story in public. The soul contract states that you now have 12 Sirius Risings left in physical form. For the first three of these you will teach the Sister who will sit where you have sat for the past 30. During the next 13 moons, you will graduate *knowing* your husband. After the third festival, you and Daniel will leave the temple grounds and journey to Marseille to meet with Binyamin. His second child, your niece, will interest you. Her daughter will be approaching womanhood at this time and the Goddess must be present in her life. The Anunnaki work tirelessly to see that this will not happen. You will spend 18 moons with the girl and return here for the Festival. You will spend the 13 moons following the sixth Rising of Sirius here, and, upon completion of the Festival, you will journey to the land of your birth. As a young girl, you vowed to stay in Judah and fight the Anunnaki. Miriyam persuaded you to join her, and here you are in Ephesus. Nevertheless, because of the unbalanced emotion you displayed in your youth, you must return to heal the karma[54] you created for yourself. You will spend 26 moons creating what you would call secret societies in honor of the Goddess. With your entanglements complete, the remaining four cycles of time will be upon you. Of this time, I shall not speak. What do you say, daughter?"

Rachel squeezed the object in her hand and knew that whatever it was, it held her upright and in complete alignment. She made no oral communication with the Crone but used her eyes to transmit her sense of peace.

"Wonderful. The Mysteries teach of 36 Holy Ones, beings who have transcended third dimensional density, yet remain in physical form. Throughout an incarnation one must realign the frequency of its physical body before making the transition from body to spirit. To do this, one must visit one of four sacred vortices upon the Garden. The City of the Great Central Sun, Shambhala, with its entrance point in the mountains of Bod, is one of these vortices. The Holy One would go there to refresh the physical matter, purifying the body from the densities of life, and completely realign the physical matter with Divine Spirit. I know you have heard stories of beings which, upon death leave with their physical bodies, which do not decay. These are the Holy Ones of which I speak."

Rachel nodded in acknowledgment.

"The Goddess calls the Holy One through one of four messengers: Dove, Eagle, Hawk, or Owl. The four messengers come with an encoding as to which vortex the Holy One will choose for realignment and purification. If the Goddess sends forth a Dove, then the Holy One has cleared itself of all entanglements within its energetic form. This Being has no remaining karma and no outstanding contracts to return to the Garden. The Holy One embraces the imprint of the Goddess. Should it choose to return to the Garden, it does so free of karma.

"If the Goddess sends forth an Eagle, then people around the Holy One will remember their connection with the Source. The message of the Eagle is the clearing of the Holy One's karmic entanglement in the imprint of the male nature.

"If the Goddess sends forth a Hawk, then the Holy One will incarnate again as a male.

"If the Goddess sends forth an Owl, then the Holy One will incarnate as a female.

"If the Holy One also sees a Crow during this

time, then it will leave earlier than originally planned, because circumstances do not allow for full completion of its tasks.

"In the last four cycles of 12, you must be mindful of what I have shared."

In the entire time the Crone had spoken, no cloud had crossed the moon. Now, as she stood breathing in the night, a cloud slowly moved across and the light began to fade. The Crone opened Rachel's palm; there was nothing in it. She moved Rachel's hand up to her own heart and said, "Remember, feel all of your feelings," then turned and vanished into the darkness.

Rachel allowed her feelings to move through her and circulate with the land as she lay upon the grass. She drifted off to sleep and returned to her body as one of the Servers gently touched her left foot. As Rachel opened her eyes, she heard the fluttering of wings as the women entered the temple. She rose, embraced the Server, and prepared herself for the initiations.

The Servers, aiding Rachel, handed each sister a vessel for water to wash her hands and face. Then each person made her way to the pool and refreshed herself. With this complete, Rachel stood facing the area in the sky where Sirius would soon be visible, placed her arms straight out from her sides, and spread her legs shoulder-width apart. Each sister imitated her. With heads held high, each was cascaded in the gentle glow of Sirius, which was followed shortly by the reddish-golden rays of Ra.

SISTERHOOD OF THE DOVE

Rachel began to sing the song of the doves and turned to greet her sisters. Hundreds of wings sounded in the air as the graceful, white birds swooped throughout the temple and returned to their perches.

"Welcome, Dove Sisters: welcome to the ways and teachings of the Goddess," Rachel spoke enthusiastically. "In seven suns the Festival of the Goddess Isis will be upon us. Prepare your families well during this time.

"Now, celebrate yourselves; it is a glorious day."

The sisters stood, released their silent voices, and began to play as children play. Several women approached Rachel, took her hand, and welcomed her into their dance.

Music filled the temple; women and children sang, danced, and played, celebrating their entrance into the Sisterhood. This lasted most of the morning, and as Ra rose to his height in the sky, the sisters gradually departed the temple through the Western Gate. The Servers tidied the area, said their good-byes, and Rachel was once again alone in the temple. As she sat near the pool, a family of deer approached for a drink of water.

Ra was low in the sky when Rachel felt prompted to leave the temple. Her mother was on her mind, and, as she readied herself to leave, she looked up at the large, black altar stone, which Joseph had brought over from Alba. It was a gift from the Druid people, and had been present for

Miriyam and Yeshua's sacred union. Somehow it was connected to the chalice from which she had drunk and which she had never seen again. It was smooth and not from this Garden, with shards of crystal in it, which glistened in the light. It kept the sisters connected to the Hathors, the Sirian's, and all of the, 'Brothers and Sisters of Light,' who chose not to incarnate in human form. When energy passed through the stone, the water beneath it was charged with whatever energy was transmitted at the time.

Rachel was about to reach up and touch the stone, when she heard Miriyam calling to her. "Rachel. Rachel, turn around." Rachel did as she was asked. Standing before her was Miriyam, who looked so real that Rachel ran to hug her before she realized Miriyam was in spirit form.

"As the Crone said, I left my body last night. I have come to say how proud I am of you. I shall always be present if you need me. I have arranged with The Council for my energy to stay close to this Garden. The soul contract of the 22 is still in effect and will be for several lifetimes to come. As long as the Anunnaki insist upon influencing this Garden with fear, greed, jealousy, power, and control, we must continue to balance their influence with love. I have spent the time cycles since leaving this temple, building another one: an energetic temple where we have anchored the Light of the Dove. In the times to come, long after you have joined me, one will come forth who will recall. This one will be known as a prophet who will collect the information we have placed in the new temple and scribe its energy into the written word that people will understand. The energy of the Dove will live on. Remember that our commitment to the soul group is greater than any commitment made within this Garden of matter." Rachel watched Miriyam's face turn from that of a Goddess teacher to that of the mother who had nurtured her into womanhood. "I have visited with Rivka, Baruch, and Sarah, and I shall visit Binyamin next. You have cared for the temple well," she said, looking around and smiling.

Rachel knew that she had.

"I visited your son and daughters before coming to visit you; all four of them are beautiful. I visited Daniel and your grandchildren as well. The seed of the Goddess lives on."

"Was your transition smooth?" Rachel asked.

"The transition is smooth or challenging as one chooses. My body suffered with illness. I placed my attention, however, upon the Dove, and birthed myself into spirit.

"Be mindful of the Anunnaki, my love, now that only three remain in body. Sarah has the Druidic Guardians to shield her. Now is the time for Daniel to manifest the Dove Guardian within himself. His last illness came about through a quickening of his DNA as the Dove merged with him upon deeper levels." Miriyam placed both of her hands over her heart, bowed, and turned. "Now let me see if I shall startle your brother," she said, looking over her shoulder and winking.

Rachel watched Miriyam walk out of the temple grounds through the Eastern Gate. She noticed that Miriyam chose not to vanish and felt that Miriyam was affirming that she might walk into Rachel's life at any moment and truly was not gone.

Rachel, full of a myriad emotions, made her way out the Gateway of the West and moved to her rest area. She packed her belongings and journeyed home to Daniel.

CHAPTER 10
FESTIVAL TIME - CYCLE THREE OF 12

Rachel ran to greet her uncle Joseph as he came up the path. She had heard that he was coming for Festival time. She had prepared a new "storyteller" for the temple and recalled the words from the Crone about her departure. Rachel felt glad to see Joseph. As they embraced, she saw Sarah standing behind him. Rachel reached out and embraced her. Sirius had risen in the sky many times since they had seen each other.

That evening Joseph sat in Rachel's home and told Sarah, Daniel, and her how Miriyam had spent her time, and of the many Goddess communities she created. Miriyam had evolved to a high level and the Dove had circled her head. She had come and asked Joseph to take her part of the way to the sacred vortex of realignment and purification, but at the time of their departure, Miriyam told him that she had made other arrangements with the Goddess. The Goddess had come to her offering a choice. She showed Miriyam that it would be more instrumental and healing for the people around her, if she would stay longer in body. Exiting life through death, however, was the price to pay for this choice. This would mean she would stay close to the Garden, and would take human form again when the time was called for, instead of ascending as Yeshua had. Joseph said that 10 harvests had come and gone since her scheduled ascension date, and that she had died of an illness.

During that time, Miriyam moved upon her path with little food and little water. She was in constant communion with the Goddess and had little interaction with people, though *they* always knew she was present. Salome, Binyamin, and Joseph were a few of those whom she allowed near her.

The night was long and Rachel treasured the stories Joseph bestowed upon them.

The next morning Sarah told Rachel of the many joys and challenges of her journey. The celibate life she had chosen posed, at one point in particular, a great challenge. The Anunnaki had come forth to her as they had to Yeshua in the Sinai. Sarah told her that she wished Yeshua had shared more than he had of those times. She recalled him saying that each person must face the shadow within themselves, and speaking of an initiation that lasted 40 suns, wishing hers had been that short. Said Sarah, "For three moons I was tested, and, like Yeshua, I must be vague. I did feel his presence, and that of the Hathors, during that time, and I graduated to the levels of teacher and guardian, and entered the inner community of the Druid."

During Sarah's travel to Ephesus at this time, she met up with Binyamin and his family. Binyamin was working with Joseph, growing affluent in a life that bridged the Goddess teachings with the world of business. He made his home in southern Gaul, near Marseille.

Binyamin showed Sarah a gift that Miriyam had left with him. She had acquired it during her time in Alba. Apparently, it was the only gift a Magus had ever given her. It was a piece of stone, the same as that upon the altar in the temple pool. Binyamin had been given specific instructions to allow the Goddess to pass it on to one of his children. As the stone passed from parent to child, it would find its way to the one for whom it was intended. Binyamin called that person the Prophet. Miriyam was clear, giving a warning that was always given when the stone was passed. "Under no circumstance, even death, may the Anunnaki take possession of this stone." Binyamin did not know what the stone was for, but understood that it was connected to all the work she had done anchoring light within this Garden and with the soul contract.

Rachel realized that her niece would receive the stone and pass it on to her daughter, and that this was connected to the 18 moons they would soon spend together.

A few suns later, Rachel informed Sarah and Joseph that she and Daniel would travel to Marseille and stay there for a time.

Twenty-one suns later, Daniel and Rachel hugged their family members good-bye, journeyed from the temple to the shore, and boarded Joseph's boat. As the boat left the harbor, she imagined that Miriyam had felt these same feelings upon her departure from Ephesus, so long ago.

CHAPTER 11
THE PILGRIMAGE - CYCLE
NINE OF 12

"I am complete, Daniel," Rachel whispered to him the morning after the Festival of Isis.

Daniel turned his face toward her and smiled. "Should I pack our things?"

"Soon, my love, we shall leave Judah. I want to see Jacob one last time."

"May I suggest we leave for Tiberias in six suns' time? I shall tie up loose ends while we stay with Jacob, and you may move as you are directed after that."

Rachel took his hand in hers and squeezed. They gazed into each other's eyes, breathed deeply, and rose out of bed.

* * * * *

Twenty-one suns after her arrival in Tiberias, Rachel was called to the River Jordan. As she sat in meditation upon the riverbank, she felt the energy of Sarah. Rachel connected upon the inner plane, as Sarah desired. She breathed deeply and elevated herself to the inner plane where Sarah waited for her.

Sarah spoke: "In a short while, even moments from now, the Sirian's will come for me. The owl flew over my head three suns ago. The Sirian's will take me to her vortex. I love you and I shall hold your seat at the Council table. Know that Joseph comes for you. Journey well, for you will see your sign before the full moon."

Rachel embraced her, kissed her upon both cheeks, returned to her body, and entered the Jordan.

A while later Rachel returned and said to Daniel, "Sarah has graduated physical form. Two Festivals ago, we said good-bye to our daughters, their children, their children's children, and to those at the temple. Now we're here to say good-bye to our son and his children. I did not anticipate saying good-bye to Sarah, as well. It hurts, Daniel. My heart hurts so much," she said, tears forming in her eyes.

"I have studied so long and still my mother was

right. Each moment we must remember that we are whole. With all of these good-byes it is easy to feel separate." Rachel began to cry and curled up in Daniel's arms. They cried together. When their tears were through, he asked, "When do we leave, my love?"

"I have not yet received the sign but Sarah said that it is near."

"I must help Jacob with his house; will you excuse me?" Rachel drew him close to her and let him go. She lay upon the warm grass and recalled the words of Miriyam. "Upon rising, one may not maintain the same attitudes from the sun before. It matters not how long one has studied the teachings or how long one has prayed. Each sun the dust of life collects upon people as it collects upon a table. As one daily cleans the table of that dust so must one clean oneself each moment while one is in this Garden. Every word that one utters, every exhalation, and each step one takes creates an energetic reaction."

Recalling her words brought Miriyam's courage back to her heart, and as she readied herself to rise, an eagle swooped down from the sky, calling her to her place of realignment and purification.

CHAPTER 12
THE PROPHET - EARLY
1500S AD

The stone wand has passed from parent to child for almost 1500 years now. The energy that incarnated as Miriyam has agreed with other Council members that Earth is ready for the next infusion of Light; the Anunnaki have moved their way into the sacred energetic temples Miriyam created. The Inquisition is unfolding upon Earth and many are about to be tested in their beliefs. Earth is holding a vibration similar to that in the days Miriyam walked upon her.

A soul group has come forth to prepare the way for the arrival of the Prophet Miriyam predicted. Within this group, three members of the soul group of 22 have chosen to incarnate a fragment of themselves. These three members were known at the time of the New Millennium as Miriyam of Migdal, and Yeshua's *brothers* Simon Peter and John. These three have volunteered a fragment of themselves to be incarnated with other fragments in three specific bodies upon Earth. The soul fragment of John birthed as the father of the Prophet. The soul fragment of Simon Peter birthed as a teacher with whom the Prophet will come to study, and the soul fragment of Miriyam birthed herself as a king of Gaul.

The soul of the Prophet during the time of the New Millennium was over-soul to John the Baptist. This soul has chosen birth in southern Gaul in the early 1500s AD. It has chosen male form as female writers of this period are frowned upon. When the time is appropriate, the mother of the Prophet, who is in possession of the stone wand, will hand it to Michel[55] and he shall scry[56] the energies of the Goddess, write them down, and preserve them for generations.

* * * * *

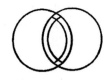

CHAPTER 13
THE RETURN OF THE 21 –
TODAY

I recommend you create an environment free of
distractions before you continue this chapter.

*Read the next two paragraphs fully; then
continue.*

*Take a deep breath into your belly and continue
breathing up into your lungs until they are full.
Release this breath with a sigh, clearing all stored,
out-of-balance energy within you.*

*Take another deep breath into your belly,
continuing it up into your lungs. Hold it as long as
possible and exhale completely, pushing every last
bit of air out of your lungs and belly. Continue*

breathing into your belly and filling your lungs, then exhale hard until you feel you have exhaled all stress.

With the stress released, breathe comfortably and continue to read while journeying in an altered state, simultaneously.

Invoke the Goddess in a form that is supportive to you. There is no right or wrong name; there is no wrong or right form of the Goddess. Choose that which empowers and supports you. For the purposes of this writing, we have chosen the Goddess form of Isis.

Feeling supported, protected, and empowered, imagine yourself in Ephesus, walking in the early morning hours to the Dove temple for your initiation. It is before sunrise on July 23; the air is warm and comforting, and Nut's starry, moonlit sky magnificently twinkles above you as you approach the Eastern Gate of the temple.

You have with you a satchel full of offerings for the animals.

The Alignment of Sirius will take place within the next two hours. This is when the Star of Sirius rises in the sky moments before sunrise, marking the beginning of the Goddess Celebration: the Festival time or the harvest time, which takes place over seven days and culminates with the Feast of Isis[57].

You begin to contemplate your initiation. It

matters not if you are currently man or woman, adult or child. You are reminded of how it feels to carry within you a fragment of a Dove Sister.

Recall now the first time you came to the temple.

Was it with Miriyam? Was it with Rachel?

Were you female? Were you male?

Were you a child? Were you an adult?

Did you help Mary, Miriyam, and others build the temple? Had the temple already been built?

Did you travel to Ephesus with Miriyam? Did you travel to Ephesus from a foreign land? Were you born in Anatolia?

Take a deep breath now as you place your foot upon the outer step of the temple and ascend the first step to the Eastern Arch, preparing yourself to enter this sacred space. Notice the temple's construction of stone used to create pillars, stairs, tiers, arches, altar, and more.

Ascend to the next step; notice the temple's attention to beauty and nature as fig and olive trees are merged into its design.

Move now to the third step, focusing your awareness upon the moonlit arches outlining its circular shape and taking in the seven other open entrances, each leading to the center of the temple, where the altar stands with its sacred pool of water.

Become aware of the outer size of the temple, made the size of the inner circumference of the base of the Great Pyramid: something Miriyam learned during her studies in the library of Alexandria.

Breathe in the temple's magnificence.

As you move through the gateway now, feel your current form shift and change to a liquid, flowing body of light; descend the three huge, circular tiers, which make their way around the entire temple. Walk over the grass to the center of the temple garden. Set your things down and kneel against the side of the raised, circular, stone pool. Place your elbows upon its edge and bring the palms of your hands together.

Move your awareness to your heart, taking a deep breath; as you do so, you hear Miriyam singing a love song to the Goddess Isis. Miriyam's song begins as a soft, sweet melody, gently increasing in volume, as the passion of her soul sings its harmony with nature.

Reach into your satchel now and pull forth an offering for the doves, the deer, and all of the creatures making their way to you.

Turn around now; locate Miriyam's chair, and begin to move toward it. Upon arriving, sit upon the grass before it. As you do, the temple begins to fill with other initiates. Miriyam appears and takes her seat. She smiles at you, and you feel a warmth move through your body.

MAITREYA ZOHAR

Miriyam begins addressing the initiates:

"What I am about to share with you, you have experienced several times. I ask you to open your ears to my words, open your soul to my sound, and open your being to the spirit of the dove which desires to fill your heart."

You watch as Miriyam rises, places her hands above her head, and calls aloud with commanding voice, "Isis, make all hearts present here this morning one heart, your heart. Make my speech, your speech." There is a thundering clap of Miriyam's hands and she returns to sitting, readying herself to infuse the spirit of the dove into all who are present. The wind picks up ever so slightly. Isis is moving through the crowd, touching each heart.

Miriyam begins speaking again:

"The Council has gathered again. Members from each region of the universe have witnessed great turmoil taking place. They speak their observations of human beings and how we have become glazed over, forgetting our origins, our connection to the Goddess, and our true abilities and possibilities.

"Much discussion happened around whether or not the peoples of Earth have called out for change. In the days of Queen Nefertiti, 44 beings volunteered and served together to bring about a shift in consciousness relating to the Anunnaki's influence of fear, jealousy, power, and control. With the poisoning of the young Tutankhamun, the Anunnaki's influence took roots and the 44 beings were guided to withdraw. I was one of those 44 beings who ventured forth during that time under a different name and a different face.

"In my life as Miriyam I volunteered again, as you have volunteered now. Before my incarnation, The Council formed a group of souls and over-souls that would respond to the call of Earth.

"Twenty-two of us formed the soul group and entered a contract to incarnate upon Earth to remind her peoples of their true origin. The other 22 formed an over-soul group, who committed themselves to watching over the 22 of us who had chosen to incarnate.

"Unlike the time of Queen Nefertiti, when the 44 birthed themselves, many of us fell into the density of Earth's vibration, forgetting who we were and why we had come. During my life as Miriyam, the 22 of us each had a counterpart in the over-soul group who supported us. This kept us connected to the Divine, allowing us to maintain our memory of who we truly were.

"The contract written by the 44 of us said that many in the soul group would come together at a particular point in time, to awaken the peoples of Earth to the teachings we had come to share. This contract also stated that with the birth of the one known as Yeshua, time as it had been measured upon Earth would change. The new time-period would be called the New Millennium.

"Members of the soul group who chose incarnation before the New Millennium would have a slightly more difficult time remembering their origin, than those of the soul group who chose to be born after the New Millennium. Those of us born after would incarnate into the consciousness already birthed upon Earth with the one you know as Yeshua. To support the members of the soul group birthed before the New Millennium, an additional 12, highly evolved beings manifested to awaken the memory of each member. They acted as the gate openers for the teachings the 22 would pass on. These highly evolved beings were called Magi. Furthermore, we chose to come knowing that once we looked into the eyes of a Magus, the memory of our soul contract would awaken, and life might seem more difficult.

"The Council arranged for the 22 of us to incarnate upon Earth at its deepest point: the Dead Sea.

"Members of The Council continue to gather to this day: February 2, when the year ends with an even number. They meet to discuss a variety of things, of which the Anunnaki's influence upon Earth is one.

"The 44 souls continue in service, balancing the affects of fear, jealousy, power, and control within the realms of Earth. Currently, many of the soul group that was 22 have agreed to send portions of themselves or soul fragments back to Earth. To affect a larger area of the world they have placed their soul fragments in many different vessels, including humans, dolphins, and whales.

"I, who was Miriyam, and the other 20 from the time of the New Millennium, have chosen to birth ourselves in many forms: different races, religions, ages, and genders.

"Our new soul contract states that most will fall under the influence of the Anunnaki; then, through understanding our shadow nature, the over-soul group and The Council will begin to ignite the soul fragments of the original 22.

"This means that 1,000s upon 1,000s will begin to awaken in a relatively short span of time, as experienced in the late 1980s when The Council arranged for an event to take place which would ignite these fragments within the 1,000s of souls that had agreed to step forward and address the influence the Anunnaki held over Earth. To many, this awakening was called the Harmonic Convergence. Since then, many gatherings have taken place to quicken the vibration of Humans from the dense vibration of fear into the light-speed vibration of love.

"As these fragments are ignited, the human beings holding them begin to magnetize toward one another. They begin to see the parallels between the times Yeshua, the other 20, and I walked upon Earth, and the conflicts and turbulence happening in that same area of the world today: the Middle East.

"The original soul group anchored the Dove energy in hiding in Ephesus, but this was not how, or where, we had originally intended. We had intended to anchor the Dove Consciousness openly in the area of the Dead Sea, the deepest point on Earth, and because of the overall resistance of the collective consciousness, a detour was created.

"The Plan has never wavered however, the Council desires to place a foundation of energy in this Middle Eastern region. Now is the time for people to open their third-eyes and unite their vision of the future.

"In order to create a new future, we must become receptacles, not aggressors. We must each become a chalice. We must each be a walking grail to receive the sweet waters of life: the nectar, allowing that to overflow and recognizing that old conditioning clogs us; it pollutes the waters of our planet; it creates confusion; creates flood or drought instead of a steady, flowing, stream.

"It saddens me to say that most of the current world leaders are still Anunnaki. There is a saying, 'Cleanliness is next to godliness.' In Hebrew, the word *anu* means *us*, and the word *naki* means *clean*: *clean us*.

"Ponder this in relation to the Anunnaki influences of fear, jealousy, power, and control that may still reside within your human form. Ponder what you feel to be the opposite of fear. Some may say courage, others may say bravery, and I shall say fun. What is the opposite of fear for you? When you find this word, write it down. Instead of spending your time focusing upon releasing fear, focus upon this new word, which is your own opposite to fear. It is the word which will liberate you from fear. Manifest the essence of this new word without reservation. Focus only upon what you desire to attract into your life.

"Now, continue this exercise with jealousy. Find your own opposite of jealousy and write it down. Your authentic self will give you the perfect word, the perfect feelings based upon your conditioning from this life and others to free yourself from the influence of the Anunnaki.

"Continue to do this exercise with the word power, calling forth from deep within its opposite for you, and write it down. Then move on to find your opposite of control, and write this down.

"When it is appropriate and preferably within the next 72 hours I recommend you write the following or something similar: In the name of Isis and with her support, I (place your name here), release and clear any and all Anunnaki influences of fear, jealousy, power, and control." Now burn this paper. Then, taking a new sheet, write out your new words and become familiar with them and what it is that you desire to create. Focus on that which you desire, not its opposite."

Feel Miriyam smiling at you as she instructs the following:

"Stand now; feel your liquid, light body radiating. Move your feet shoulder width apart; raise your arms to the sky with palms upward. Face the direction of Sirius; she is rising above the horizon. Now, drink in her essence as she bathes you with unconditional love.

"Now, bring your hands to your heart and bow to the light within me as I bow to the light within you.

"It brightens my 'heart' and the 'hearts' of 1,000,000s to welcome you into the Sisterhood of Dove. Receive the grail I am offering you now. Drink deeply of its nectar of life, that you may be freed of the influence of fear and begin to attract and experience (your word); that you may be freed from the influence of jealousy and begin to attract and experience (your word); that you may be freed from the influence of power and begin to attract and experience (your word); and that you may be freed from the influence of control and begin to attract and experience (your word) in every moment of your daily life.

"Know that my presence is ever near and that you are loved beyond all measure.

"Go forth and celebrate yourself during this Festive Time and always.

"RA BA RA. This translates as: Light, Soul or Spirit, Light.

"The Goddess lives in you always. We are always connected. We are one."

CHAPTER 14
A NEW BEGINNING

You are the visionary, writer, director, and actor/actress of your own life. Scribe the new journey you desire. Scribe what you envision your life to be:

a. In one years time.

b. In three years time.

c. In five years time.

d. In 10 years time.

Referring to the preface, as you read Sisterhood of the Dove a minimum of three times and listen to it once:

1. What did you receive from on the first reading?

2. What did you receive from the second reading? How have you shifted yourself?

3. What did you receive from the third reading?

4. What did you receive from listening? How have you changed your paradigm?

ABOUT THE AUTHOR

Early in 1987, Maitreya met world-renowned psychic and spiritual teacher Shoshana/Ortalia Rogers, an encounter which sent him on a new spiritual path, one that would take him from Toronto to Brooklyn and finally to Los Angeles, California, to pursue his metaphysical career.

Along the way he became ordained as a minister with the Universal Brotherhood Movement, Inc.

Maitreya currently serves as a channel, psychic, healer, metaphysical teacher, and ionCleanse practitioner.

You may visit him on the Web at

MAITREYA ZOHAR

www.myspace.com/maitreyazohar or E-mail him at
SisterhoodOfTheDove@gmail.com

ABOUT THE CHANNEL OF MARY MAGDALENE

Shoshana/Ortalia was born in Tel Aviv and since childhood maintained her divine connection. As a psychic, healer, and metaphysical teacher she offers one on one sessions, initiations, and life changing classes for over 23 years.

Ordained as an Interfaith Minister in 1987 Ortalia is a "genius of insight, compassion, and clarity."

Ortalia currently makes her home in Brooklyn,

New York when she is not travelling the world in service to the Earth.

To discover more please visit www.GoddessOnCall.byregion.net or email SOAR221@aol.com or SOAR221@gmail.com

Workshop & Initiation
Awakening Your Inner Dove

Has Mary's mission and life of service touched
you?
Do you yearn to reconnect with the masters?
The Dove Sisters and the Soul Group of 44 are
currently incarnated in numerous men and women.
The door is open to embracing your fear, jealousy,
power, and control; awakening your inner dove.
Reawaken into the Order of the Dove.
Reconnect and call forth your sacred symbol.
Discover the impact you make in the universe.

For details on this workshop and others visit:
www.myspace.com/maitreyazohar

To register:
E-mail: SisterhoodOfTheDove@gmail.com

Also Available:
Sisterhood of the Dove is available as an eBook
through
www.outskirtspress.com/SisterhoodOfTheDove

In the works:
Audio Book
Divination Cards

For information on upcoming Global Healing and
Self-discovery Journeys visit:
www.myspace.com/maitreyazohar

Chapter 1 - Advent

[1] Ephesus – located in Turkey.

[2] Judah – located in Israel.

[3] Festival(s) – this term relates to the annual harvest and celebration times and marks the cycle of a passing year.

[4] Anatolia – Turkey.

[5] Soul Group of 22 – listed in alphabetical order; name definitions adapted from http://www.behindthename.com; the author added the Lesson, Zodiac, Balance & Imbalanced Qualities to the name deifinitions; the 22 would later become known as:

ANDREW (apostle of Jesus) – From the Greek name Andreas, which derives from aner "man" (genitive andros "of a man"). In the New Testament, the apostle Andrew was the brother of the apostle Simon Peter. According to legend he was crucified on an X-shaped cross.

Lesson: nurturance

Zodiac Sign: Cancer

Balanced Qualities: modeling the merger of masculine and feminine nature; preparing a sacred space; care and nurturance of the physical body

Imbalanced Qualities: attachment to a home as a physical place

BARTHOLOMEW (apostle of Jesus) – From Bartholomaios, this was the Greek form of an Aramaic name meaning "son of Talmai." Talmai is a Hebrew name meaning "furrowed." In the New Testament Bartholomew was an apostle also known as Nathaniel. NATHANAEL – From the Hebrew name Nethane'el, which meant, "God has given." In the New Testament, this is the name of an apostle also known as Bartholomew.

Lesson: balance

Zodiac Sign: Libra

Balanced Qualities: true balance; going under the surface; preparing people for something new; clarity; humor; charm

Imbalanced Qualities: cutting; overbearing; manipulative in a negative way; responding to others with little tact

ELIZABETH (wife of Zechariah and mother of John the Baptist) – From Elisabet, the Greek form of the Hebrew name Elisheba meaning "God is my oath." In the New Testament, this is the name of the mother of John the Baptist.

JAMES (brother and apostle of Jesus) – English form of the Latin Jacomus, which was derived from Iakobos, the New Testament Greek form of Ya'aqob (see JACOB). JACOB – From the Latin Jacobus, which was from the Greek Iakobos, which was from the Hebrew, name Ya'aqob, which meant "holder of the heel" or "supplanter."

Lesson: flexibility

Zodiac Sign: Gemini

Balanced Qualities: yield one's personality to the Will of God

Imbalanced Qualities: confusion; multiple personalities with different ideas

JAMES (apostle of Jesus and brother of the apostle John) – English form of the Late Latin Jacomus, which was derived from Iakobos, the New Testament Greek form of Ya'aqob (see JACOB). According to the Book of Acts Herod Agrippa beheaded him. JACOB – From the Latin Jacobus, which was from the Greek Iakobos, which was from the Hebrew, name Ya'aqob, which meant "holder of the heel" or "supplanter."

Lesson: philosophy

Zodiac Sign: Sagittarius

Balanced Qualities: expressive; honest; traveler; justice

Imbalanced Qualities: hold onto ideals tightly, to the point of losing all perspective; narrow-minded; may act in a way not considering the consequences

JESUS (called Yeshua in this story, husband of Miriyam, father of Sarah, Rachel and Binyamin; Jesus of Nazareth, Jesus Christ) – English form of Iesous, which was the Greek form of the Aramaic name Yeshua. Yeshua is itself a contracted form of Yehoshua (see JOSHUA). Yeshua ben Yoseph, better known as Jesus Christ, was the central figure of the New Testament and the source of the Christian religion. JOSHUA – From the Hebrew name Yehoshua, which meant, "YAHWEH is salvation." The name Jesus was a variant of the name Joshua. YAHWEH – A name of the Hebrew God, represented in Hebrew by the tetragrammaton ("four letters") Yod He Waw He, transliterated into Roman script Y H W H. Because it was considered blasphemous to utter the name of God, it was only written and never spoken. This resulted in the original pronunciation being lost. The name may have originally been derived from the old Semitic root hwy meaning "to be, to become."

JOHN – (John the Baptist) – English form of Johannes, which was the Latin form of the Greek name Ioannes, itself derived from the Hebrew name Yochanan meaning "YAHWEH is gracious." Herod Antipas beheaded John the Baptist, the forerunner of Jesus Christ.

JOHN (apostle of Jesus and brother of the apostle James)– English form of Johannes, which was the Latin form of the Greek name Ioannes, itself derived from the Hebrew name Yochanan meaning "YAHWEH is gracious." John is the supposed author of the fourth Gospel and Revelation.

Lesson: Courage

Zodiac Sign: Leo

Balanced Qualities: gracious, merciful, and compassionate heart

Imbalanced Qualities: pride, boasting, and taking glory for the self rather than giving glory to the Lord

JOSEPH (Joseph of Arimathea; uncle of Jesus) – From the Latin Josephus, which was from the Greek Iosephos, which was from the Hebrew name Yoseph meaning "he will add."

JUDAS (cousin and apostle of Jesus) – Greek form of JUDAH. JUDAH – From the Hebrew name Yehudah, which meant "praised." Popular belief has it that Judas Iscariot betrayed Jesus.

Lesson: vision

Zodiac Sign: Pisces

Balanced Qualities: playfulness; strength; laughter; vision; foresight; willingness to speak with anyone about anything; depth of spirit; Neptunian dreamer like qualities

Imbalanced Qualities: jealousy; competition; favoritism; suicidal

MARY (mother of Jesus) – Usual English form of Maria, which was the Latin form of the New Testament Greek names Mariam or Maria (the spellings are interchangeable), which were from the Hebrew name Miriam. The meaning is not known for certain, but there are several theories including "sea of bitterness," "rebelliousness," and "wished for child." However, it was most likely originally an Egyptian name, perhaps derived in part from mry "beloved" or mr "love."

MARY (called Miriyam in this story, wife of Yeshua, mother of Rivka, Baruch, Sarah, Rachel and Binyamin; Mary Magdalene) – Usual English form of Maria, which was the Latin form of the

New Testament Greek names Mariam or Maria (the spellings are interchangeable), which were from the Hebrew name Miriam. The meaning is not known for certain, but there are several theories including "sea of bitterness," "rebelliousness," and "wished for child." However, it was most likely originally an Egyptian name, perhaps derived in part from mry "beloved" or mr "love."

MATTHEW (apostle of Jesus) – English form of Matthaios, which was a Greek form of the Hebrew name Mattithyahu which meant "gift of YAHWEH." Matthew supposedly authored the first Gospel in the New Testament.

Lesson: responsibility

Zodiac Sign: Capricorn

Balanced Qualities: offers people the opportunity to give

Imbalanced Qualities: being one of many faces – acting one way while believing another; creating power struggles amongst people; working excessively

PAUL (substitute apostle of Jesus, filled in the void left by Judas) – From the Roman family name Paulus, which meant "small" or "humble" in Latin. Saint Paul was an important leader of the early Christian church, his story is told in the Book of Acts in the New Testament. His original name was Saul, and upon converting to Christianity changed his name. He authored most of the epistles in the New Testament.

PHILIP (apostle of Jesus) – From the Greek name Philippos which means "friend of horses", composed of the elements philos "friend" and hippos "horse."

Lesson: organization

Zodiac Sign: Virgo

Balanced Qualities: organized thoughts; teach power of the mind to create; enquiring; asking questions; inquisitive

Imbalanced Qualities: disorganized, busy mind; unfriendly; a loner

SARAH (first born daughter of Yeshua and Miriyam) – Means "lady" or "princess" in Hebrew.

SIMON (apostle of Jesus known as Simon the Canaan) – From the Greek form of the Hebrew name Shim'on, which meant, "hearkening," or "listening."

Lesson: dependability

Zodiac Sign: Taurus

Balanced Qualities: faith in God; heed the Will of God

Imbalanced Qualities: fighting governments; materialism; security; acquisition; money

SIMON PETER (apostle of Jesus) – From the Greek for of the Hebrew name Shim'on, which meant, "hearkening," or "listening." The New Testament presents Simon, also known as Peter (a name given to him by Jesus), as the most important of the apostles. Simon Peter was the most prominent of the apostles during Jesus' ministry. He was considered by some to be the first pope. PETER – Derived from Greek petros meaning "stone." In the New Testament Jesus gave the apostle Simon the name Cephas (meaning "stone" in Aramaic) which was translated Peter in many versions of the Bible.

Lesson: initiative

Zodiac Sign: Aries

Balanced Qualities: listen to G-D's initiative; unshakeable; immovable

Imbalanced Qualities: self-involved; easily persuaded

THADDEUS (apostle of Jesus) – Possibly means "heart" in Aramaic.

Lesson: community

Zodiac: Aquarius

Balanced Qualities: share with others how to unite and commune with their heart and the global heart

Imbalanced Qualities: rude; tactless; uncertainty; looking toward one's own personal gain; change mind to fit in with the crowd

THOMAS (apostle of Jesus) – Greek form of the Aramaic name Te'oma, which meant, "twin." In the New Testament, he was the apostle who doubted the resurrected Jesus. According to tradition, he was martyred in India.

Lesson: transformation

Zodiac Sign: Scorpio

Balanced Qualities: intuitive; commune with spirit; gift of healing

Imbalanced Qualities: doubt; lack of faith; suspicion; self deceiving

RACHEL (second born daughter of Yeshua and Miriyam) – Means "ewe" in Hebrew. Ewe – the female of the sheep especially when mature.

ZECHARIAH (husband of Elizabeth and father of John the Baptist) – From the Hebrew name Zekaryah, which meant, "YAHWEH remembers." Zechariah was temporarily made dumb because of his disbelief.

[6] The tearing of his clothes is an expression of, "You are dead to me, my daughter is no long alive, I will mourn the death of my daughter."

[7] Litter – a wheelless vehicle for transporting of people.

[8] Garden – Planet Earth; the Earth plane or consciousness of Earth.

[9] Ima – Hebrew for mom or mother.

[10] Salt Sea – the Dead Sea.

Chapter 2 – Sacred Union
[11] Desire – the author of this text has not once used this word with the definition of lust or anything of the lower nature. Desire in this context is not to be confused with needing or wanting. True desire is of Spirit. Spirit moves its Will through the energy of desire. Much of man's lower nature is

driven by his needs and wants before he ascends to his/her inner Spirit's desire.

¹² <u>Morning Star</u> – Venus.

¹³ <u>Alba</u> – one of the Celtic Nations, currently named Scotland.

¹⁴ <u>Stone Circle</u> – the standing stones of Callanais, located on the Isle of Lewis, Scotland.

¹⁵ <u>Place of the Dove</u> – Isle of Iona, Scotland.

¹⁶ <u>Peaked Island</u> – Isle of Arran, Scotland.

¹⁷ The Magi were not of Earth consciousness. They would travel back and forth on ships; they did not need to birth themselves as they were evolved far beyond the cycles of birth, death, and rebirth. The Magi would manifest or materialize a body when the soul contract so called for it. They would materialize bodies in the likeness of physical beings that were currently on Earth, such as kings, so they might have power and free access to travel without anyone questioning them.

¹⁸ <u>Sirius</u> – the brightest star in the night-time sky, located in the constellation Canis Major. The Ancient Egyptians based their calendar on the heliacal rising of Sirius, which occurred just before the annual flooding of the Nile.

Sirius was nicknamed the Dog Star and this is where we get the phrase "the dog days of summer" from.

The Dogon tribe of Africa are reported to have astronomical knowledge of Sirius that would normally be considered impossible without the use of telescopes.

[19] The site of Miriyam and Yeshua's sacred union saw the currently standing Christian Church named Rosslyn Chapel, built in 1446, built on it.

[20] The chalice was last in the Holy Temple during the time of King Solomon.

[21] Gaul – France.

[22] Sirius Alignment – this is the name given to the time (early morning of July 23) that the star of Sirius rises in the sky just before the sun does.

Chapter 3 – The Making of a Priestess

[23] Great Sea – Mediterranean Sea

[24] Aur River – Nile River.

[25] Elementals – these beings present themselves in numerous forms of which some are fairies, gnomes, elves, sprites, pixies, etc.

[26] Thunder Beings – spirits of Thunder, Lightening, Wind, and Rain.

[27] Humility – bowing one's personality or ego self down to the Light of the Divine within one self.

[28] Pesach – Passover

Chapter 4 – Miriyam's Vision Begins

[29] Queen Nefertiti, King Akhenaten, and Tutankhamun were all part of the 18th Egyptian Dynasty.

[30] The Kinneret – Sea of Galilee

[31] We may judge the apostles as being the character traits that were their challenge, or we may look at them as part of the soul group that was serving the mass consciousness by choosing to manifest the shadow side within themselves, to teach the world. Also worth considering, is the fact that the soul contract needed to be carried out. If the 11 had come forth, betraying the soul contract, then they would have been tried, convicted, and crucified alongside Yeshua. The Anunnaki would have scored a major victory if this had happened. It is therefore wise to remember that at times, the Divine uses our flaws in service of ourselves, others, and the higher good.

[32] Psalms – The 10 Psalms Jesus recited were Psalm numbers: 91, 67, 30, 33, 111, 112, 133, 100, 124, 150

[33] Tikunim – tikkun olam is a Hebrew phrase, which translates to "repairing the world."

Chapter 7 – The Dove Returns

[34] Phoenicia – Lebanon.

[35] Atlantis –an advanced civilization that thrived for many thousands of years. Its exact end time is unknown, but it was somewhere around 12,000 years ago, when Earth shifted on its axis.

[36] Land of Buddha – China.

[37] Land of the Rising Sun – Japan.

[38] Land of the Red Man – North America.

[39] Landmass – South America.

[40] Southern part of the northern Landmass –
Mexico.

[41] Central portion of the northern Landmass –
United States of America.

[42] Upper part of the Northern Landmass –
Canada.

[43] <u>Lakes</u> – Great Lakes – Lake Superior, Lake
Michigan, Lake Huron, Lake Erie, Lake Ontario.

[44] <u>Mountains</u> – Jasper National Park, Canada.

[45] Land of Krishna – India.

[46] She is referring to an elephant.

[47] <u>Bod</u> – Tibet.

[48] She is referring to a llama.

[49] She is referring to the Aboriginal peoples of
Australia.

[50] She is referring to a kangaroo.

Chapter 8 – Secret Societies

[51] <u>Eire</u> – Ireland

[52] Today this sacred energetic Line is known
by many as: el Camino.

[53] The Way of St. James, often known by its
Spanish name, el Camino de Santiago, is the
pilgrimage to the Cathedral of Santiago de
Compostela in Galicia in northwestern Spain. It is
said that the remains of the apostle Saint James are
buried there.

Chapter 9 – Welcoming the Dove

[54] <u>Karma</u> – a Sanskit word describing the concept of "action" or "deed" denoting the entire cycle of cause and effect described in Hindu and Buddhist philosophies. Karma is a sum of all that an individual has done, is currently doing, and will do.

If one believes in reincarnation, then karma extends through the present life and all past and future lives as well and has an accumulative effect.

Chapter 12 – The Prophet

[55] <u>Michel</u> – Michel de Nostredame, his latinised name, lived from December 14, 1503 – July 2, 1566 and became known as Nostradamus. He is one of the world's most famous publishers of prophecies.

[56] <u>Scrying</u> – an occult practice of using a medium (polished stones, crystals, mirrors, water) as a form of divination to aid one's psychic abilities.

Chapter 13 – The Return of the 21

[57] <u>Feast of Isis</u> – the Egyptian calendar was made up of 12 months of 30 days each, and five days were added at the end. These five days are known as the Feast Days honoring Osiris, Horus, Set, Isis, and Nephythes. The rising of the Nile, the crucial event in the Egyptian agricultural cycle, was predicted by the heliacal rising of Sirius. Isis's feast day is on July 30, exactly seven days after the annual helical rising of Sirius, which is on July 23.

Lightning Source UK Ltd.
Milton Keynes UK
UKOW051036270412

191593UK00001B/10/P